Mrs. H. Howson

Home Cookery

Mrs. H. Howson

Home Cookery

ISBN/EAN: 9783744789158

Printed in Europe, USA, Canada, Australia, Japan

Cover: Foto ©Lupo / pixelio.de

More available books at **www.hansebooks.com**

HOME COOKERY.

250 TESTED RECEIPTS.

BY MRS. H.

SECOND EDITION.

PREFACE.

This cookery book bases its claim to the attention of the housewife on the fact that each receipt has been practically tested in the ordinary course of household affairs and has met the approval of more than one competent judge.

The number of receipts has been purposely limited, in order that no one may have the least difficulty in finding and choosing a dish, and that there may yet be a sufficient variety to please the most capricious taste.

Mrs. H.

November, 1880.

CONTENTS.

	PAGE
SOUPS	5
SHELL FISH	14
FISH	18
MEATS	20
GAME AND POULTRY	29
MADE DISHES	32
VEGETABLES	43
SALADS	46
BREAKFAST AND TEA CAKES	48
SAUCES	51
PASTRY	56
PUDDINGS	61
DISHES FOR DESSERT	71
PLAIN SWEET CAKES	78
FANCY CAKES	86
PRESERVES, JELLIES, BEVERAGES, CANDIES, ETC.	89
PICKLES	96
POTTING	98

WEIGHTS AND MEASURES.

AVOIRDUPOIS WEIGHT.

16 drams .... 1 ounce.
16 ounces .... 1 pound.
28 pounds .... 1 quarter of hundred.
4 quarters, or 112 pounds .... 1 hundred.
20 hundred. .... 1 ton.

LIQUID MEASURE.

4 gills .... 1 pint.
2 pints .... 1 quart.
4 quarts .... 1 gallon.
63 gallons .... 1 hogshead.
2 hogsheads .... 1 pipe or butt.
2 pipes .... 1 tun.

DRY MEASURE, FOR GRAIN, FRUIT AND POTATOES.

2 pints .... 1 quart.
8 quarts .... 1 peck.
4 pecks .... 1 bushel.
8 bushels .... 1 quarter.

The following approximation of weights may be useful to housekeepers not having scales:

Wheat flour, one qt. is one lb.
Indian corn, one qt. is one lb. one oz.
Butter, when soft, one qt. is one lb. one oz.
Loaf sugar, broken, one qt. is one lb.
White sugar, powdered, one qt. is one lb. one oz.
Best brown sugar, one qt. is one lb. two oz.
Eggs, (average size,) ten eggs are one lb.
Sixteen large tablespoonfuls make a half-pint,
    and eight make a gill.

INDEX TO ADVERTISEMENTS.

		PAGE
Allen & Bro.	Furniture	106
Barrett & Marshall	Hardware	109
Bendimere, F.	China repaired	112
Borden & Bro.	Ventilators	106
Brown, C.	Groceries	102
Bush, F. M.	Upholsterer	103 & 107
Bush Hill	Second-Hand Store	112
Carrick, David, & Co.	Crackers	110
Chillman, P. E.	Photographer	107
Continental Carpet Cleaning Works		111
Cook & Bro.	Hosiery	4
Davis, A.	Butcher	102
Earle & Sons	Picture Galleries	115
Grieb, J. L.	Tailor	111
Hamrick & Son	Jewelers	109
Harlan, T. H.	Groceries	101
Harman, J. C.	Umbrellas	101
Howell & Bourke	Paper Hangings	108
Howson & Sons	Patents	115
Hutchison, H.	Apothecary	107
Jarrett, B. F.	Groceries	117
Knowles, L. & Co.	Flour	116
Lutz, G. L.	Tailor	107
Matthews & Co.	Stationery	101
McCallum, Crease & Sloan	Carpetings	114
Medlar, A. J. Co.	Crackers	102
Paxson, Comfort & Co.	Monuments	114
Schoch, H. J.	Livery Stables	116
Schwartz, G. A.	Toys	112
Sichel, J.	Millinery	107
Slack, J.	Groceries	110
Sutherland, William	Gardener	102
Stewart, Pierce & Co.	Notions	104
Strawbridge & Clothier	Dry Goods	113
Thackara, Buck & Co.	Gas Fixtures	111
Toy & Bro.	Plumbing	110
Vandegrift, C. M.	Hardware	116
Wanamaker, J. & Co.	Clothing	108
Wanamaker, John	Grand Depot	105
Wiener Bros.	Fruiters	104
Willimantic Co.	Spool Cotton	109
Wood, S. C.	Confectionery	106

COOK & BROTHER,

51 & 53 North Eighth Street,

PHILADELPHIA,

Are the largest Retail dealers in Hosiery and Underwear in America.

Our Importations embrace the productions of every manufacturer of reputation in

ENGLAND,
    SCOTLAND,
        IRELAND,
            FRANCE,
                SWITZERLAND, and
                    GERMANY.

While our Domestic Department represents the Products of

Twenty First-class Mills,

Our Stock is unequalled anywhere in the great essentials of

VARIETY,
      AMOUNT, and
           CHEAPNESS.

SOUPS.

CARAMEL FOR COLORING SOUPS
AND GRAVIES.

One pound of brown sugar, one pint of cold water; put sugar in a perfectly dry saucepan, and when it changes color, add a little cold water to cool the sugar, then add the rest of the water; as soon as it boils, take from the fire, and it is then ready for use.   D.

ASPARAGUS SOUP.
ONE HOUR.

Boil a bunch of asparagus until quite soft; in another saucepan boil some milk; thicken it with flour and quarter-pound of butter; season with pepper and salt; and just before serving, strain the water from the asparagus on the milk and flour and butter; then serve.

BEAN SOUP.

Two pounds of salt pork, four quarts of water, a quart of beans; add a teaspoonful of soda. Let the beans boil until the hulls will easily slip off; take them out and throw them in cold water; rub well with the hands—the hulls will rise to the top—drain carefully, and repeat until the hulls are removed; put the beans back in the pot with the pork. Season with pepper, salt, thyme, some potatoes cut small, and grated carrot. Cut toast in pieces and put in the tureen.

BEEF TEA.

Take one pound of beef, remove the fat and cut it up in very small pieces, and cut up one bunch of celery, or a teaspoonful of celery-seed, and a very small red pepper; pour on one pint of cold water, and let it stand two hours; then take out the pepper, and put the saucepan on the range and let the tea simmer slowly two hours. Strain it before giving it to the patient.

BLACK OR TURTLE BEAN SOUP.

Take one quart of beans and soak for twenty-four hours before cooking. Take the remains of a roast of beef, as free from fat as possible, or two pounds of beef and one pound of salt pork—this is better than the ribs, as it flavors the soup better. Boil together in a large pot, in six or eight quarts of water, first adding six onions, cut up fine. Boil the whole for five hours. Mash and strain out the bean-skins; flavor with a bunch of herbs, thyme and celery; pepper and salt to taste; add a half-pint of wine to a tureen of soup. Put in six or eight hard boiled eggs, and serve with lemon.

CLAM SOUP.

Put a quart of clams, with their liquor, on the fire with a pint of water; boil them about three minutes, during which skim them well, then strain them and remove the soft portions of the clams and keep them warm; return the liquor to the fire, with the hard portions of the clams, half an onion, a sprig of thyme, three or four sprigs of parsley, and one large blade of mace; cover it and let it simmer for half an hour. In the meantime put three ounces of butter into a stewpan, and when it bubbles sprinkle in two ounces or one heaping tablespoonful of flour; stir it on the fire until cooked, and then stir in gradually a pint of hot cream or milk; add this to the clam liquor (strained), with a seasoning of salt and a little cayenne pepper, also the soft clams, without chopping them. When well mixed, and thoroughly hot (without boiling) serve immediately.

CONSOMMÉ SOUP.

TIME, 4 HOURS AND HALF.

Boil three pounds of meat in five pints of water four hours; let it cool. Then remove the fat from the stock; pour the stock into the boiler and let it get hot; then separate the whites of two eggs—add to the whites a little salt and pepper and half-gill of cold water; then beat them up. When the stock gets tepid, throw in the whites of the eggs and seasoning, with the shells; stir up with two forks. The instant it boils, the egg rises to the top and takes off imperfections. Then, when it has boiled about three minutes, pour it through a clean kitchen towel. A little browning should be used to color it. Boil some turnips and carrots about ten minutes, and put them in the tureen, and pour the stock over it.

CORN SOUP.

Clean and scrape twelve ears of corn; boil the cobs fifteen minutes in one quart of water—remove them and put in the corn; let it boil a short time, then add two quarts of milk; season with pepper and salt; butter that has been melted enough to rub two tablespoonfuls of flour. Let the whole boil ten minutes, then turn the soup into a tureen, in which have been placed the yolks of three beaten eggs; stir well and serve.

GREEN PEA SOUP.

Take a knuckle of veal, cut it in pieces and put it in a soup-kettle with four quarts of water; boil it moderately fast and skim it well; when the meat is boiled to rags strain it out and put in the liquor a quart of green peas—they must be young. Boil them until dissolved, and till they have thickened the soup and given it a green color; have ready two quarts of green peas that have been boiled in another pot, and if liked, a sprig of mint and a teaspoonful of sugar, (which will greatly improve the taste); after they have boiled in this pot twenty minutes, take out the mint, put the whole peas into the pot of soup, and boil all together ten minutes, then put it into a tureen and serve.

LOBSTER SOUP.

The foundation should be made of fish, or any white stock whether of fish or meat answers perfectly well. Take care that all the fat is removed from the stock. Let it boil, and add two or three tablespoonfuls of flour; stir it over the fire until it thickens, then put in two ounces of butter—when dissolved, beat in the yolks of two eggs, and stir moderately for ten minutes; withdraw the stewpan to the side of the range, so that it will keep simmering. Put in the soup a canned lobster, or a fresh boiled lobster; let it cook ten minutes.

MOCK-TURTLE or CALF'S-HEAD SOUP.

Take the liquor the calf's head was boiled in and put in four sliced potatoes, three turnips, two carrots, one small onion—all cut fine—some chopped parsley, sweet marjoram, thyme, some celery-seed, pepper pod and salt; after it has well boiled, strain through a cullender; then mix two tablespoonfuls of flour and one of butter smooth, and add to the soup, with one teaspoonful of caramel. Let it boil again; if not seasoned enough, add more; have three hard-boiled eggs—mash the yolks and put them in the tureen, and pour the soup over them; add a half-pint of wine. Make force meat balls of minced veal and beef suet, in equal quantities; season with pepper and salt, sweet herbs, nutmeg and mace, and some beaten yolk of egg to make all these ingredients stick together; flour your hands, and make up in balls—flour the balls well and fry in butter; put some in the soup, or send them to table on a separate dish.

OKRA GUMBO.

Cut up one chicken—an old one is preferable; wash and dry it; flour it well, add salt and pepper; have ready in a saucepan a lump of lard the size of an egg—let it get hot; then put in the chicken; fry it brown all over, but do not let it burn; put it in the vessel in which you make soup; pour on it five quarts of water, let it boil two hours, then cut up about two okra pods and add them to it—be sure they are tender; then let it boil another hour. When you first put on the soup cut up an onion in it, salt and pepper to taste. To be served with rice. Dried Okra can be used if soaked over night.

ORIENTAL MULLAGATAWNY SOUP.

Cut up a chicken, put it into a soup-kettle, with a small sliced onion, carrot, celery, parsley, three cloves, a very little cayenne pepper, some salt; cover it with four quarts of water; add any pieces of veal, with the bones—of course a knuckle of veal would be the proper thing; add a quarter of a cup of rice. When the pieces of chicken are nearly done take them out, and trim them neatly to serve with the soup. Let the veal continue to simmer for three hours. Now fry an onion, a small carrot, and a stick of celery sliced, in a little butter; when they are a light brown throw in a tablespoonful of flour; stir it on the fire one or two minutes, then add a good teaspoonful of curry powder, and the chicken and veal broth; place this on the fire to simmer for an hour; half-an-hour before dinner strain the soup, skim off the fat, return it to the fire with the pieces of chicken and two or three table-spoonfuls of whole boiled rice. This will give time enough to cook the chicken thoroughly.

OX-TAIL SOUP.

Take three ox-tails—these will make a large tureen of soup; ask your butcher to divide them at the joints; rub them with salt and put them to soak in warm water while you prepare the vegetables—three stalks of celery, two carrots, two turnips, two onions, a bunch of savory herbs, a teaspoonful of pepper-corns; three quarts of water. Put the ox-tails in soup-kettle, with an ounce of butter, the vegetables, and a half-pint of cold water; stir it over the fire for a short time, until the pan is covered with a glaze, then pour in the three quarts of water. Skim it well, and simmer slowly for four hours, or until the tails are tender; take them out, strain the soup, stir in a little flour to thicken it; add a glass of port-wine, a half-head of celery previously boiled and cut in small pieces; put the pieces of tail in the kettle of strained soup; boil it up for a few minutes and serve.

This soup can be served clear by omitting the flour, and adding to it the carrots and turnips cut in fancy shapes, with a head of celery in slices. These may be boiled in a little of the soup, and put into the tureen before sending to table.

OYSTER SOUP.

One pint of oysters, with liquor, half-pint of milk, three ounces of butter, an ounce of flour, pepper and salt, and grain of cayenne pepper. First strain the liquor well from the oysters, then put it on the fire and allow it to boil; skim it very carefully; then melt the butter in a separate saucepan and stir in the ounce of flour; when they are mixed, add the milk and stir it until it boils, then add the liquor, and let them boil together for two minutes; then add the oysters, pepper and salt, and boil for another minute.

PEA SOUP.

Wash the pea pods and put them in the kettle; cover with cold water, and let them boil for two hours; strain; put back the water into the kettle, and enough milk to make as much soup as you wish, but not enough to make it look white; mash some cooked peas through the cullender, and thicken with a little flour. Add butter, salt and pepper, to taste. The water in which the peas have been boiled will increase the strength of the soup if added.

PEPPER POT

Take four pounds of tripe and a set of calf's-feet; put them into a large pot with as much water as will cover them; some whole pepper and a little salt. Put them on the fire early in the morning; let them boil slowly, keeping the pot closely covered. When the tripe is quite tender, and the feet boiled to pieces, take them out and skim the liquid and strain it—then cut the tripe into small pieces, put it back into the pot and pour the soup or liquor over it. Have ready some sweet herbs, chopped fine, some sliced onion and some sliced potatoes, and season them with pepper and salt; make some small dumplings with flour and lard or butter; put the vegetables into the pot, add a large piece of butter rolled in flour, and lastly put in the dumplings; boil till the ingredients are thoroughly done, and then serve it up in a tureen.

SPLIT PEA SOUP.

(From an Old Gentleman's Diary of 1777.)

Take one quart of split peas, put to them five quarts of cold water, quarter of an ounce of Jamaica pepper, two large onions, one pickled herring (washed in two or three waters and the roes out) skinned and cut to pieces. Boil all together till a quart is diminished. Pour in a pint of boiling water, and let the whole boil a quarter of an hour; take it off and strain it through a cullender; throw into the soup seven or eight heads of celery, three heads of endive—all of them cut very small—together with a handful of dried mint, passed through a lawn sieve. Set all these on the fire and boil the whole near three-quarters of an hour, stirring the soup perpetually to prevent burning, which it will do in a moment, and therefore the pot should stand on a trivet. Bread cut small and fried crisp in butter must be thrown into the soup; then serve.

SPLIT PEA SOUP.

FOUR HOURS.

Soak one quart of split peas over night; in the morning take three pounds of beef, a coarse piece will do, put it in the soup pot with the peas, add four quarts of water; boil gently for three hours, skimming it well, then put in a small onion cut up, some thyme, pepper and salt. It must be boiled till the peas are entirely dissolved, then strain it, and serve it up with toasted bread cut in small squares.

TURKISH SOUP.

Take one quart of stock, one tablespoonful of cream, pepper and salt; first wash half teacupful of rice; then put stock and rice in a saucepan, allow them to boil twenty minutes; after boiling, rub through a sieve with a masher, and then return to the saucepan; drop into a basin the yolks of two eggs—add to the eggs one tablespoonful of cream, and mix them up; then take a large spoonful of stock and put on the egg and cream, then add all the stock and put it on the fire.

SHELL FISH.

CLAM FRITTERS.

Wash the clams in two waters, chop them fine; add pepper and some chopped parsley; beat three eggs up very light and add to the clams; stir in a half pint of cream, slowly dredge in some flour until it is of the consistency of fritters; have the pan hot, and put in half butter and half lard, as in frying oysters—let it boil, and drop in a spoonful of the fritter batter. As soon as browned, serve hot.

TO CHOOSE AND PREPARE CRABS.

The heaviest crabs are usually considered the best. Have a pot of boiling water; put the crabs in and cook for half an hour; they are usually eaten cold. A very nice way is to open them and take off the spongy part, remove the sand-bag and head—they are near together—empty the shell and pick the meat from the crab and large claws and put it back in the shell; or mix the meat with a very little oil, vinegar, salt, black and cayenne pepper to your taste, and some hard boiled eggs, chopped up; replace it in the large shell and put in the oven to brown.

DEVILLED CRABS.

Take twenty-four crabs, plunge them into boiling water and boil half an hour; break open the crab-shells; reject the poisonous parts and pick carefully from the inner shell, and save the coral colored shells to cook in. Make a dressing of one tablespoonful of butter and one of flour; place the flour and butter together in a stew-pan; put over the fire and braid together; then add three eggs, beaten, one teacup of milk, and season with cayenne pepper and salt. Mix this dressing well with the crabs; place it in the shells to bake, first scattering bread-crumbs over the top, and small bits of butter. Bake ten minutes.

SOFT SHELL CRABS.

These crabs must be cooked directly, as they will not keep till next day. Remove the spongy substance from each side of the crab and also the little sand-bag; put some lard and butter into a pan; when it is boiling hot put the crabs in it; after you take them out throw in a handful of parsley and let it crisp, but withdraw it before it loses its color; strew it over the crabs when you dish them. If you wish gravy, make it by adding cream or milk to the butter, with some chopped parsley, pepper and salt; let them all boil together for a few minutes, and serve in a sauce-boat.

TO BOIL LOBSTER.

The heaviest are the best. Put them, alive, into a kettle of boiling water, which has been salted, and let them boil from half-an-hour to three-quarters, according to their size; when done take them out of the kettle, wipe them clean, and rub the shell with a little salad oil, which will give a clear, red appearance; crack the large claws without mashing them, and with a sharp knife split the body and tail from end to end. Send to table and dress in any way preferred.

FRIED OYSTERS.

To one dozen of large oysters, take three eggs, one pint of milk; beat the eggs first, then pour in the milk and mix well; season with cayenne pepper and salt; drain the oysters perfectly dry; first lay them in bread-crumbs, then in cracker-dust; have the fat boiling hot, but be careful not to let it burn, and fry them a light brown; when one panful is fried strain the fat and use it again.

STEWED OYSTERS.

To one dozen of oysters, one large teacupful of milk, piece of butter not quite the size of an egg; season with salt and pepper—cayenne is better; put on to cook, and stir until they come to a boil, when they are ready to be served.

PICKLED OYSTERS.

Take one hundred oysters, drain off the liquor, cover them with boiling water, stir and cook about three minutes; take them off of the range and stand away to cool; then take enough vinegar to cover them, and put in a teaspoonful of whole cloves—salt and cayenne pepper and black pepper to taste; put it on to boil five minutes; after it comes to a boil then add a little of the liquor that the oysters were cooked in; when both are cool put the oysters in the spiced vinegar.

STEWED SNAPPER.

Cut the head off a snapper, then hang the snapper up for several hours; then put it in a pan of hot water; wash it well, and break the shell and take out the meat—be careful of the gall—and put the meat in a pot with a very little water, the same as you would to stew a chicken; when tender, make a dressing of milk, a large piece of butter, some allspice, mace, pepper and salt, some flour to thicken it, yolk of one raw egg; when done, add wine.

PREPARED TERRAPINS.

Put the terrapins alive in boiling water, for three minutes, one by one, then take them out and take off the skin of the feet; then put them in a fresh pot of boiling water, with some salt; let them boil for half-an-hour, or until they are tender; break open the shell, use all the meat but the head; be careful and not break the gall and the sand-bag, which are to be found in the liver; use about half of the liver, mixed smooth with flour and cream, the balance of the liver cut up with the meat. To each terrapin use a quarter-pound of butter, some cayenne pepper and salt, some ground allspice, and a small quantity of mace. To a half-dozen of terrapins take the yolks of four eggs, well beaten; add to the terrapins after they are taken from the fire; then add wine to the taste, or about half-pint to six terrapins.

FISH.

TO BROIL FISH.

Rub the bars of your gridiron with drippings, or a piece of beef suet, to prevent the fish from sticking to it. Put a good sized piece of butter into a dish, work into it enough salt and pepper to season the fish—lay the fish on it when it is broiled, and with a knife-blade put the butter over every part; serve very hot.

TO FRY FISH PLAIN.

When the fish are cleaned and washed, dry them well with a cloth, and lay them out singly; flour them, and season with pepper and salt, and fry them brown, in plenty of good drippings; serve with parsley.

FISH À LA RUSSE.

Half-pound flour, quarter-pound of butter, one teaspoonful of Royal Yeast Powder, three eggs, one teacupful of boiled rice, one pound of fish of any kind, one gill and a half of cold water, and a little pepper and salt.

First boil two eggs ten minutes, then separate the yolk from the white of a raw egg, add to the white a pinch of salt, then beat it up light; take the flour, add the yeast powder, then the salt, the white of the egg, and one and a half gills of water, or more or less water according to the flour. After it is kneaded, roll out as thin as possible, then weigh quarter-pound of butter, and divide in three pieces—cut one piece and spread it over the dough, and fold it in three, and so on until you use all; roll it as square as possible, then beat up the yolks of the eggs and brush round the side of the dough; then put the boiled rice in the middle of the dough, the boiled eggs over the rice, and salt and pepper, and then the fish having the bones taken out; then fold the crust over it all, brush the crust with the yolk of egg, then put it in a floured pan and cook for half-hour. Garnish with parsley. D.

CODFISH BALLS.

Soak the fish over night, then boil about two hours, and then pick very carefully all the little bones out; boil some potatoes, and mash through the cullender so as to avoid lumps; have equal quantities of fish and potatoes; season with red pepper to taste; chop up hard boiled eggs in drawn butter, and mix through it; make up in small cakes, and fry brown.

BOILED SALMON.

Take some fresh salmon, put it in a napkin, and boil it a half-hour; have drawn butter made with hard boiled eggs chopped up, and put in, with chopped parsley.

MEATS.

ROAST BEEF.

A three-rib roast of beef, weighing twelve pounds, will require two hours and a half to cook it, rare. Put it in a clean dripping-pan, without water; do not season it, but baste it every quarter of an hour with its own drippings; when done, remove it from the pan and strain off the drippings; pour some back in the pan, put it on the range and dredge some flour in, and add pepper and salt; stir until it is smooth and brown, then pour some hot water in and cook for a few minutes. Serve in a sauce-boat, hot.

YORKSHIRE PUDDING, which may be baked and served with it, is made with one pint of milk, three eggs, four tablespoonfuls of flour, pinch of salt, beaten to a thin batter; pour in the pan, when the meat is half-done, and when baked, remove with the meat.

À LA MODE BEEF.

Select a piece of the round of about eight pounds, remove the meat around the bone carefully, keeping it whole as possible; cut strips half-an-inch in width and the depth of the meat in length, of uncooked corned pork; run these strips into the beef from the top to the bottom, so that in slicing the meat it will cut nicely, and the more introduced the better the flavor. Then mix together one tablespoonful of ground allspice, one teaspoonful of cloves, five blades of mace, one tablespoonful of summer savory, one tablespoonful of sweet marjoram, one tablespoonful of ginger, one tablespoonful of salt; then make incisions in the beef and introduce through it the above articles, well mixed together. This must be prepared the day before it is cooked, to allow of the flavor being communicated to the beef. Lay in the bottom of the stewpan some pieces of corned pork cut in thin slices; on this lay the beef, having tied it tightly around with tape to keep it in good form; then make a little bunch of thyme and parsley, and lay it on the beef; slice two onions, scatter them over the beef, then pour over it one quart of cold water, and set this aside to simmer very slowly for four hours. It must be cooked with care, and kept tightly covered. Half-hour before dishing, pour off the gravy and skim all the fat off; strain it, and add a wineglassful of mushroom catsup to half-pint of gravy, and stir in a spoonful of flour to thicken it; let this simmer for a few minutes only, then pour it over the beef, removing the herbs and onions from the top, as they must not be served.

FILLET OF BEEF.

Three pounds of the fillet of beef; lard it by sticking a knife through different parts, in which put slices of fat salt pork, about half-inch wide and three long; then tie it in shape with twine, and put it in a baking-pan; in the bottom put some pork or suet; sprinkle pepper and salt, and put a large ladle of hot stock or boiling water in the pan; baste it often. It will take about forty minutes to cook it. Make a gravy of some stock, add some mushrooms, pepper and salt and caramel to brown it.

FILLET OF BEEF WITH SAUCE.

Cut the beef in slices about an inch thick; rub the gridiron with butter, and put the beef on, and then over the fire for seven minutes, and then put it on the dish and put Dutch sauce around it. To make the sauce, take half-tablespoonful of cream, yolks of two eggs, one ounce of butter, pepper and salt, juice of half-lemon. Put in the saucepan half-tablespoon of water, the yolks of the eggs, the lemon, the cream, the butter; now whisk these over the fire, but do not let it burn; when hot, draw it to one side and serve. D.

SALTING BEEF.

Take eight pounds of coarse salt, four gallons of water, two ounces of saltpetre, three gills of molasses.

ROAST OX HEART.

Take a fresh ox heart, clean it and remove the gristle; make a stuffing of sage and onions, a little cayenne, salt and black pepper; sew up the opening and roast for two hours, basting it well; make a nice gravy, and serve, with apple-sauce.

STEWED OX HEART.

Take a fresh ox heart, clean it and remove the gristle; make a stuffing of two large spoonfuls of finely chopped beef suet, three large spoonfuls of bread-crumbs, a little finely powdered summer savory and thyme, a little cayenne; then lard the heart well with strips of fat corned pork; lay some slices of corned pork in the bottom of a stew-pan; stuff the opening of the heart well, sew it up, and lay it in the stew-pan, with twelve allspice and twelve pepper-corns and two bay-leaves; pour on one pint and a half of cold water; cover the pot closely, and let simmer very slowly for two hours; then make a rich sauce: rub some flour and butter together, and on it pour from the stew-pan half-pint of the gravy, one large spoonful of mushroom catsup, and let this simmer; pour some over the heart when dished, and send the remainder to the table in a sauce-boat. Serve hot.

TO FRY BEEF KIDNEY.

Take a beef kidney, cut it in thin slices, let them soak in warm water for two hours, changing the water twice to thoroughly cleanse the kidney; dredge a very little flour over these slices, and fry them a nice brown in about three ounces of butter, seasoning them with pepper and salt. Make a small quantity of gravy, and serve.

TONGUE STEWED.

Get a beef's head and tongue from the butcher—the tongue to be stewed, and the head to be boiled with the tongue; the liquor to be kept for stock.

ROLLED TONGUE.

While a boiled tongue is still warm, roll it, with the tip inside, and place it in a round tin just large enough to hold it in place; let it stand over night, when it will remain rolled after being removed from the pan. Serve it whole, on a bed of salad, or water-cress or parsley.

WINDHAM CUTLETS.

Four or five mutton cutlets—half-ounce of butter, pepper and salt, a small carrot and a piece of turnip, sprig of parsley, nearly a pound of mashed potatoes, yolks of two eggs; put in a small frying-pan the butter; when hot, cook the cutlets in this butter for five minutes, on each side; cut the carrot and turnip into small pieces, then put them in boiling water and cook them for twenty minutes, then the potatoes; put them in a saucepan, add pepper and salt, the yolks of two eggs; put on the fire and stir until the eggs are dry, then put it aside until ready for use. Flour the board slightly; cut a small quantity of potato and roll the cutlet in it; then flour slightly a baking-pan; then brush them with a little egg or milk; then brown them in the oven, quicker the better; then, after adding the brown sauce, the cutlets are ready. Make a pile of the vegetables in the middle, to embellish the dish. D.

BROILED SHOULDER OF LAMB.

Get a shoulder of lamb boned from the butcher; press it for broiling; place the gridiron over a clear fire, and rub the bars with butter to prevent the meat from adhering to them; put the lamb on the gridiron, and turn it frequently; when cooked, have a hot dish with a large lump of butter, pepper and salt; when the butter is melted, put the lamb in the dish, and serve at once. Garnish with parsley.

BREADED VEAL CUTLETS.

Have the cutlets cut from the fillet about three-fourths of an inch thick, and about as large as the palm of your hand; grate some stale bread and rub through a cullender, and adding salt, pepper, sweet marjoram, grated rind of a lemon, a little powdered mace and grated nutmeg, spread this on a large flat dish; beat up some eggs, dipping each cutlet into them, then into the prepared bread, seeing that a sufficient quantity adheres to each side of the meat; have boiling some sweet lard, and a small quantity of butter added, in which fry your cutlets, turning them three times, but be careful they do not burn. Place in a hot and covered dish; make a gravy by sifting flour into the fat in the pan, stirring until a rich brown, when add boiling water, to form the right consistency; add, lastly, a little chopped parsley and vinegar, and pour, boiling, over the cutlets. Serve at once.

FRICANDEAU OF VEAL.

Three or four pounds of the fillet of veal, a few slices of bacon, a bunch of savory herbs, two blades of mace, two bay leaves, five allspice, one head of celery, one carrot, one turnip, lardoons, pepper to taste, one pint of gravy or stock.

Cut a thick handsome slice from a fillet of veal, trim it neatly round and lard it thickly with fat bacon; cut the carrot, turnip and celery into slices, and put them into a stew-pan with a bunch of savory herbs, two blades of mace, five allspice and two bay-leaves, with some slices of bacon on top. Lay the fricandeau over the bacon with the larded side uppermost, dust a little salt over it, and pour around it a pint of good gravy or broth. Place it over the fire and let it boil, then let it simmer very gently for two hours and a half or three hours over a slow fire, basting it frequently with the gravy. Take out the fricandeau when done; skim off the fat, strain the gravy and boil it quickly to a strong glaze, cover the fricandeau with it, and serve it up very hot, upon a dish of green peas.

ROLLED VEAL.

Take a boned breast of veal, lay it on the dish, spread over it a dressing made of bread-crumbs, a small onion, sweet marjoram, pepper and salt, a lump of butter, and over that fifty oysters; roll it up and tie around tightly, and put it in a pan and bake one hour. Make a gravy of some pieces of veal and stock.

TO PREPARE A CALF'S HEAD.

Have the butcher split the head and take out the eyes, remove the teeth and gums; then lay it in a large pan of warm water to disgorge; then remove the brains and tongue; take the head, wash it well and put it in a pot with a knuckle of veal, and water enough to cover it; let it boil slowly for four hours, skimming it well; take out the head and veal, and dress it as you like, or bake it according to receipt. The brains you soak in cold water, with salt, for one hour; separate the lobes of the brain with a knife before you soak them; then cover with hot water and parboil them, and fry or stew them, as you like. The tongue is to be boiled, then skinned; take off the roots, and lay it on a dish; garnish with parsley. The liquor the head is boiled in save for soup.

BAKED CALF'S HEAD.

Boil the head until you can pick all the bones out, and keep the water the head is boiled in; take the pieces and lay them in a dish, having cut them small; use some salt, pepper, a little parsley, a grating of nutmeg, a small piece of butter, and some dry bread-crumbs, about a teacupful; moisten it all with some of the water the head was boiled in; put in a baking-dish and let bake for a half-hour. Take the yolks of two eggs and make a sauce with the boiled liquor. Make soup of the rest of the liquor.

TO ROAST A CALF'S LIVER.

Wash thoroughly and wipe dry; cut a long deep hole in the side; stuff with crumbs, bacon and chopped onions, salt and pepper to taste, a piece of butter, and one egg. Sew or tie together the liver, lard it over, and bake in the oven, basting frequently. Serve with gravy and currant jelly.

STEWED CALF'S LIVER.

Boil the heart and haslet in enough cold water to cover them; add three onions; while they are boiling, prepare the calf's liver by cutting incisions into it, in which put strips of corned pork cut narrow—the more it is larded with pork the better will be the flavor. Put into the stew-pan a quarter-pound of butter; when melted and boiling hot, add a teaspoonful of flour; stir until a light-brown color, then place in the liver, turning it over and around until it is cooked on all sides. Lay a small bunch of summer savory, parsley, a bayleaf, salt, a few pepper-corns, a half-dozen allspice, five whole cloves, a squeeze of lemon in the pan, and when heart and haslet are sufficiently cooked, then pour the gravy over the liver and simmer slowly for an hour and a half, the pan being tightly covered; then pour off the gravy, strain it, and add one tablespoonful of mushroom catsup or a wine-glass of wine; add a tablespoonful of flour to thicken the gravy, and boil for five minutes. Put the liver in a dish and pour some of the gravy over it; the remainder send to table in a sauce-boat. This is a delicious dish, if carefully prepared.

TO ROAST A SUCKING PIG.

Begin your preparations by making the stuffing. Have four good sized boiled and mashed potatoes; while they are hot, stir in a lump of butter the size of a walnut; boil three onions—mash them with the potatoes; add pepper and salt, tablespoonful of finely rubbed sage. When well mixed, stuff the pig, after you have washed it well in cold water, and cut off the feet close to the joints, leaving some skin all round to fold over the ends. Take out the liver and heart, and reserve them, with the feet, to make gravy. Truss back the legs. Fill the body with the stuffing—it must be quite full—and then sew it up or tie it round with buttered twine; rub the outside all over with lard—this prevents the blistering of the skin. Baste well while roasting, and just before it is done rub it over with a feather dipped in olive oil; then drain the gravy from the pan—put it in a saucepan, skim off all the fat; mix a large spoonful of flour with the liver. Cut up the heart and liver fine, add pepper and salt, and let it all simmer fifteen minutes; add a teaspoonful of caramel. Serve up in a tureen with the pig. Apple-sauce is always eaten with pork.

GAME AND POULTRY.

VENISON STEAKS.

Place the gridiron over the fire, and rub the bars with butter, and place the venison on it for a few minutes; have ready a hot dish with butter, pepper and salt, and currant jelly melted in it; put the venison in it, turn it over so as to get the gravy all over it; serve with currant jelly.

Or else have the venison steaks uncooked on the table, and a lighted chaffing-dish, and put the venison in and cook with currant jelly, pepper and salt, and butter.

JUGGED HARE OR RABBIT.

Skin a hare or rabbit and cut it in pieces; dredge it with flour and fry a nice brown in butter, seasoning it with a little pepper, salt and cayenne. Make about a pint and a half of gravy, from beef; put the pieces of hare into a jar, add one onion stuck with four or five cloves; cover the jar closely to keep in the steam; put it in a deep stew-pan of cold water and let it boil four hours—if it is young three hours will be sufficient. When done take it out of the jar and shake it over the fire for a few minutes, adding a teaspoonful of mushroom catsup, two glasses of wine and a piece of butter rolled in flour, with some fried force meat balls. Serve with red currant jelly.

SPRING CHICKENS.

Split the young spring chickens down the back—as for broiling; wash and dry them very carefully; dredge them with flour, and put them in the oven; when brown, dress them with melted butter, pepper and salt.

ROAST DUCKS.

Ducks should always hang for one day, and even longer, if the weather be sufficiently cold to allow it. Stuff one of them with sage and onion, pepper and salt; season the inside of the other with pepper and salt; put them in the oven and baste them constantly until done. A short time before serving dredge over them a little flour and baste them with butter to make them brown. Serve them very hot, and pour round (not over them) a little good brown gravy. Serve some in a gravy-boat. Serve apple sauce.

WILD DUCKS AND TEAL.

You must be very particular in not roasting these birds too much—teal about twenty minutes, with a good fire; baste them very frequently, have ready a little hot butter and juice of a lemon, cayenne pepper, a glass of port wine; pour it all hot, the last minute, over your teal; the remainder left of these birds the next day makes excellent hash, taking care of all the gravy that may remain, to stew with it.

WILD DUCKS.—These birds require clean plucking and washing, which may be done by pouring warm water through the bodies after they have been drawn. Half an hour with a brisk fire will suffice to roast them; stuffing is not required. When they are sent to table, the breasts should be sliced, and a lemon be squeezed over them. Currant jelly must be served with them.

TO TRUSS A QUAIL.

A quail must be plucked, singed and drawn; then the wings cut off at the first pinion, leaving the feet, and a skewer passed through the pinions and the wings. Other fowl can in be trussed in the same way.

TO COOK A QUAIL.

Take six quail, nicely picked and cleaned; truss them; put a small piece of butter rolled in flour and a little pepper and salt inside of each bird, and put them in a stew-pan with a little water; cover them closely, so that none of the steam escapes; let them stew gently for an hour, then take them out and make a rich gravy of the liquid they were stewed in, and send them to table with bits of toast placed round the dish.

MADE DISHES.

FRENCH OMELETTE.

One pint of milk, half-pint of bread-crumbs, three eggs, half-tablespoonful of flour, one small onion chopped very fine, some chopped parsley—season with pepper and salt; beat the eggs light, and mix all the ingredients together; have melted butter in a pan, hot, and pour the mixture in; when brown, turn over double, and serve.

SCRAMBLED EGGS.

Put a small piece of butter in an earthen saucepan, and when it is melted turn the saucepan round, so that the butter will run on the sides; then break the eggs in it and put it on the range, and don't stir them until the whites are set, then gently stir all together, add pepper and salt, and serve.

MACCARONI, WITH CHEESE.

Three ounces of egg maccaroni, three ounces of grated Parmesan cheese, a little salt, a grain of cayenne pepper, half-gill of cream, one egg, one ounce of butter. Put the maccaroni in a saucepan with enough cold water to cover it; put it on the fire and let it boil a quarter of an hour; then pour the water from the maccaroni, and pour over it a half-pint of milk; let it boil twenty minutes. Whisk the egg and cream up lightly, then mix two ounces of cheese with the egg and cream, and half-ounce of butter and seasoning; pour this custard over the maccaroni; then sprinkle the other ounce of grated cheese over it, and half-ounce of butter in small pieces, and some bread-crumbs; put in the oven for ten minutes.

CHICKEN CROQUETTES.

Two sweetbreads, boiled, one teacupful of boiled chicken hashed, one boiled onion, one teacupful of boiled bread and milk, quarter-pound of butter, salt and pepper. Chop chicken and sweetbreads very fine; mix in well the other ingredients; shape into rolls, then dip in the yolk of an egg, then in cracker-dust; drop into boiling lard, and fry brown.

RICE CROQUETTES.

Half-pound of rice, two eggs, two ounces of sugar, one quart of milk, teaspoonful of vanilla, three tablespoonfuls of bread-crumbs. First boil the rice and milk twenty minutes, then add (when cold) the yolks of two eggs, then one ounce of sugar, and vanilla; mix the remaining ounce of sugar with the bread-crumbs. Flour the board slightly, roll tablespoonfuls of rice each into a small cone, then beat up the whites of eggs, into which roll the cones, then in bread-crumbs; fry in lard two minutes. This makes six balls. D.

RICE CROQUETTES FOR MEATS.

Wash and scald a quarter-pound of rice; put it in a saucepan with a half-teaspoonful of salt, some very thinly pared lemon-peel, a tablespoonful of butter; on this pour one pint of cold water, half-pint of milk, and stir it well for a moment only, then set it on a hot place to cook slowly. When the rice becomes quite soft remove it, and stir in the well-beaten yolks of four eggs; do not allow this to cook, but keep it hot while stirring it; then pour this on a tin sheet or flat surface, spread it out equally and let it cool; then divide it in portions two inches long and one inch wide—roll these into scrolls or oblong balls; dip each into bread-crumbs, and fry them a nice brown. Serve hot.

POTATO CROQUETTES.

Take one pound and a half of potatoes, tablespoonful of cream, two eggs, half-ounce of butter, grain of cayenne pepper, three tablespoonfuls of bread-crumbs, pepper and salt. First put in a pan butter and cream; stir over a fire until melted, then add seasoning and potatoes, after they have been passed through a sieve; drop in the yolks of two eggs—stir until the yolks are dried, then take off the fire; flour the board; take tablespoonful of the mixture and form in long squares about an inch thick; put on a paper bread-crumbs, then cover the croquettes with the whites of eggs, and roll them in the crumbs; smooth over with a knife, then fry them in hot fat two minutes; then take them out, put them on paper to drain, and serve.

VEAL CROQUETTES.

Mince the lean part of the veal very fine. Take two cupfuls of veal and teacupful of boiled bread and milk, with a small quantity of parsley and celery boiled in it, also a small piece of butter. Chop a very small piece of onion and a little mace and mix with the meat, and season with salt and pepper. Roll in the form of a sugar-loaf, and dip in cracker-dust and egg, and boil in lard like doughnuts.

SWEETBREADS (French Style).

Take two sweetbreads, put them into hot water, and let them boil ten minutes; when cool, skin but do not break them; season with salt and pepper, and dredge over a little flour, then fry them slowly in butter a light brown on both sides; when done place them on a dish, and remove all the brown particles from the pan (retaining the butter); then pour in, while on the fire, one gill of boiling water, and dredge in one dessert-spoonful of flour and a little caramel, stirring it all the time; then season with salt and pepper, to taste; mix well, and just before removing it from the fire, stir in gradually two tablespoonfuls of Madeira wine.

SWEETBREADS WITH PEAS.

Lay the sweetbreads in cold water for a short time, then parboil them; take them out of the water, and take off all the skin, then put them in a saucepan and boil them tender; make a cream sauce, season with pepper and salt; have some green peas, boiled, and seasoned; put the sweetbreads on a hot dish, and the peas around them; pour over the cream sauce. Serve at once.

LARDED SWEETBREADS.

Parboil three or four sweetbreads; this should be done as soon as they are brought in, as few things spoil more rapidly. When half-boiled lay them in cold water; prepare a force meat of grated bread, butter, and pepper and salt and nutmeg, lemon-peel, mixed with beaten yolk of egg; cut open the sweetbreads and stuff them with it, fastening them afterwards with a skewer, or tying them round with pack-thread; have ready some strips of bacon-fat, and some slips of lemon-peel cut about the thickness of small straws; lard the sweetbreads with them in alternate rows of bacon and lemon-peel, drawing them through with a larding-needle; then put them in the oven to brown. Serve them with gravy flavored with a glass of Madeira, and enriched with beaten yolk of egg stirred in at the last.

TRIPE.

Wash thoroughly in cold water; let it soak over night, or for several hours; put it on to cook in hot water, and boil three or four hours, till perfectly tender; cut in squares of three or four inches; put vinegar over it, and let it lay over night, and then fry.

FRIED TRIPE.

Boil tripe until perfectly tender, then cut it in pieces about three inches square; then dip them in cracker-dust and egg, and fry a nice brown in butter and lard mixed; take out the tripe and strain the fat; be sure it is not burned; then put it back in the pan and add cream or good milk; let it boil up, and season with pepper and salt. Put the tripe on the dish, and pour the gravy over it, and serve.

TO RE-COOK COLD TURKEY.

Cut up the remains of a turkey in small pieces; add to this a half-pint of oysters, cut in pieces. Strew the bottom of a deep dish with cracker-crumbs—cover with a layer of turkey and a layer of oysters, add a very little salt, cayenne pepper and mace. Repeat until the turkey and oysters are used up. Add a little liquor from the oysters, and set them in the oven for twenty minutes; then add more oyster liquor, an egg beaten, a few lumps of butter, some cracker-crumbs, and a grating of nutmeg. Let it brown nicely.

TURKEY SCALLOPED.

TIME ONE HOUR.

Pick the meat from cold turkey, chop it fine; put a layer of bread-crumbs on the bottom of a buttered dish, moisten them with a little milk, then a layer of turkey, with some of the filling, and some butter, pepper and salt, then another layer of crumbs, and so on, until the dish is full; add a small quantity of hot water to the cold gravy and pour it over the dish; then take two eggs, two tablespoonfuls of milk, one of melted butter, salt, cracker-crumbs as much as will make it thick enough to spread on the top with a knife; put bits of butter all over it; cover with a plate; bake three-quarters of an hour. About ten minutes before serving, remove the plate and let the turkey brown. Use more turkey and very little bread.

BROILED BEEF DEVILLED.

Cut slices of cold cooked beef about half an inch thick; trim them to an even size; spread them with melted butter, mixed thick with mustard and pepper and salt; dip them in cracker or bread-crumbs, rolled and sifted; put them between the bars of a double gridiron which has been buttered, and just color them over the fire. Serve them with a little gravy under them.

BEEF CAKES.

Take the part of beef used for steaks, cut it into pieces, then beat it well in a marble mortar until it is very fine— take especial pains to free it from all bits of skin and fat— then add to it good beef suet, well chopped, in the proportion of a quarter of a pound of suet to each pound of meat; season to your taste with mace, cloves, nutmeg, pepper and salt, and also thyme, sweet marjoram and parsley chopped; to these add one good sized onion finely minced; blend the whole mass very thoroughly, and make into small cakes and fry them over a brisk fire. If the meat is fresh, and you make it in winter, this will keep good for a fortnight, if pressed closely down in a jar.

CANNELURE OF BEEF.

Chop half a pound of lean cooked beef fine; rub smooth in a mortar quarter of a pound of raw fat bacon or ham fat;

ERRATUM.

MINCED VEAL.

"Three-quarters of a pound of veal," should read "Three and a half pounds of veal."

grate the yellow rind of one lemon; mix all these together thoroughly, press them together in the form of a roll, wrap the roll in buttered paper, and bake it for twenty minutes in a moderate oven. When it is done remove the paper without breaking the roll, and serve it either on a bed of parsley or lettuce, or with half-pint of any brown sauce or meat gravy.

MINCED VEAL.

Take three quarters of a pound of veal, chop fine, add three well beaten eggs, one and a half tablespoonfuls of salt, one of black pepper, one grated nutmeg, four small crackers rolled fine, three tablespoonfuls of cream, piece of butter the size of an egg; stir well together, and make in the form of a loaf. Bake it in the dripping-pan for two hours, basting it with gravy.

PRESSED VEAL.

Mince some cold boiled or cooked veal very fine; add pepper and salt and sweet marjoram, and cracker-dust or mashed potatoes, and two eggs beaten; mix all together, and roll into a form and bake, basting well.

HASHED LIVER.

Take two pounds of liver—boil it until tender; then chop up (but not too fine) five hard boiled eggs, the yolks mashed smooth and the whites chopped up fine; put them in the liver, and boiling water, enough to make the gravy; put it on the fire, and when it comes to a boil, rub a tablespoonful of flour in nearly a quarter-pound of butter, and stir into the liver. Season to taste, with salt, black and cayenne pepper, allspice and cloves to color it. It is improved by adding wine. It should be seasoned highly.

MALINA PIE.

Take cold mutton or veal, chop it very finely; then to one pint of minced meat, stir in the yolks of four well-beaten eggs, the juice of one lemon, and the rind grated; two small onions, very finely chopped, half of a nutmeg, two large spoonfuls of mushroom catsup, a very little cayenne, and salt to taste; mix this well together, and cut up into very small pieces a half-quarter of a pound of butter and stir through it; then line a dish with good paste, and put this in to bake until it is a nice brown. Serve with a nice gravy made of the bones of the cold meats. This is a very good dish.

BRAIN CAKES.

Calves' brains are a very delicate and nutritious article of food. They should be soaked in cold water for one hour, then boiled for five minutes in water with salt and vinegar; they may be then sliced and fried or stewed in gravy. For brain cakes they should be beaten to a paste, and mixed with eggs to a stiff batter; this is to be seasoned highly, with a little cayenne pepper and black pepper, salt and powdered herbs—sweet marjoram and thyme—and then fried in plenty of lard, smoking hot. They must be taken up on a skimmer when brown, and laid on kitchen paper for a moment to free them from fat. Serve either plain or with a brown gravy. They can be fried on a greased griddle.

CORN FRITTERS.

Take twelve ears of corn, score down the middle; then scrape off all the corn, till nothing remains but the hulls; put in a little salt, one cup of milk, and flour enough to make a batter, something thicker than for flannel cakes. Now separate the whites of the eggs, and beat them until they are very light; put the yolks in first, stirring without beating; then the whites. Drop the batter from a spoon into the pan of hot lard. When the fritters are brown on one side, turn them quickly for the other side to brown. Serve immediately.

CORN OYSTERS.

To one quart of grated corn add three eggs, three grated crackers; beat well, and season with salt and pepper; fry in butter and lard; drop in the pan with a spoon.

CORN PUDDING.

One can of corn, or the corn off a dozen ears, one pint of milk and three eggs, tablespoonful of flour, pepper and salt to taste, a few pieces of butter placed on the top. Bake half an hour.

PORK AND BEANS.

Soak one pint of picked beans, over night, in plenty of water; then boil them until they are quite soft, but not broken. Put a half-pound of salt pork in a pudding-dish and put the beans around it; cover closely; set it in a warm oven, and bake for half a day.

MACCARONI CHEESE.

Boil the maccaroni over night in milk, so that it very thoroughly swells, and lay it in rather a deep dish you intend to serve it in; make a custard of milk and two eggs, well beaten, gradually stirring in the cheese, which should be half Parmesan and half Chedder, very dry; add some pepper. Pour the custard over the maccaroni; bake in a quick oven, and serve hot.

VEGETABLES.

LYONNAISE POTATOES.

Slice half-pound of cold potatoes; put butter, about the size of an egg, into a saucepan; when hot, throw in two ounces of onion, minced fine; fry a light color; add the potatoes, turning them until they are thoroughly heated and a bright color; then mix in minced parsley. The potato slices should be merely moistened with butter. Serve hot.

POTATO CHIPS.

Peel and slice some potatoes very thin, and wash and drain them dry; have plenty of lard in the pan, and when boiling hot, put the potatoes in and fry a light brown; take them out and drain them on a wire sieve, and serve hot. Strain the fat, and keep it for another time.

BAKED TOMATOES.

Take large firm tomatoes, cut out the stems; make a dressing of bread-crumbs, some chopped onion, pepper and salt, a good sized lump of butter—mix well together—add sweet marjoram, and fill the tomatoes with the dressing; put some butter in a pan, place them in it, and put them in the oven, and cook half an hour, or until they are soft, but not broken. Serve on a hot dish, with the gravy from the pan over them.

STEWED MUSHROOMS.

Select fresh mushrooms. To test if they are good, drop a silver spoon in the saucepan while they are cooking; if right, the spoon is untarnished—if not, it becomes blackened. Put them into a saucepan with salt and pepper, and a very little water; let them simmer slowly; when nearly done, add a good lump of butter and a small quantity of cream. Serve hot.

TO BOIL CAULIFLOWERS.

Select such cauliflowers as are compact and white; pick off the decayed leaves, and cut the stalk off flat at the bottom; then put them, with the heads downwards, in strong salt and water for an hour, to remove all the insects. Drain them in a cullender, and put them into a saucepan with plenty of boiling water; keep the pan uncovered, and boil them quickly until tender—about twenty minutes. Skim the water clean, and when done take them up with a slicer, and serve with a cream sauce—(a drawn butter made with cream, instead of water.) Don't put in the butter until you are ready to serve, for it will curdle.

TO BOIL JERUSALEM ARTICHOKES.

Wash the artichokes very clean; peel and cut them round; put them in a saucepan of cold water, with salt. They will take about twenty minutes from the time the water boils to become tender. When done, drain them and serve with white sauce or melted butter poured over them.

EGG-PLANT.

Slice the egg-plant an eighth of an inch in thickness, pare, and sprinkle salt over it an hour before cooking; press, so as to drain off all the water. Beat up the yolk of an egg, dip the slices first in the egg and then in cracker-dust; have the lard very hot, and fry them a nice brown.

Or, cut them very thin, pare and sprinkle salt over them, and press as above, and fry a nice brown in plenty of hot lard. Serve at once.

BOILED HOMINY.

Wash and soak the hominy over night. Early the next morning, put it on to cook in plenty of water, with a little salt. It absorbs, like rice, much water, and must be cooked with care, and be perfectly white and soft. When quite done, stir in some new milk and butter, and let it stew for ten minutes. Serve hot.

SALADS.

LAWLER'S DRESSING.

Half-tablespoonful of English mustard, quarter-teaspoonful of salt, one yolk of an egg, one teaspoonful of water, two gills or a quarter of a bottle of oil, quarter of a cruet of vinegar, one dessert-spoonful of cream; sprinkle with red pepper, and stir in. In mixing, always stir in one direction and constantly. Pour the oil in very slowly, and mix in the order given; the first four articles should be thoroughly incorporated before the oil is added.

CHICKEN SALAD.

To two chickens, take ten eggs; take the yolks' of four eggs (raw), and beat one tablespoonful of oil in the yolks by degrees; boil hard the remaining six eggs; mix the yolks fine, and add to the raw eggs; add the juice of half a lemon, mustard, cayenne pepper, and salt, to suit the taste. Use about one bunch of celery to the meat of two chickens, cut up, and mix with the dressing. The hard whites of the eggs may be chopped fine and mixed in the salad.

LOBSTER SALAD.

Boil in salt and water for half an hour. Let it get cold, and pick off all the meat. Use the same dressing as for chicken salad, with vinegar according to taste.

POTATO SALAD.

Cut a dozen cold boiled potatoes in thin slices, and mix them thoroughly, with a little onion, chopped fine, a teaspoonful of salad oil, a half-gill of vinegar, and teaspoonful of parsley.

COLE SLAUGH.

Put into a saucepan one teacupful of vinegar, and let it come to a boil; then add a teacupful of cream, with the yolks of two eggs beaten in; let these boil also, and then pour it immediately over the cut cabbage, which must be seasoned with pepper and salt.

BREAKFAST & TEA CAKES.

BREAKFAST CAKES.

One pint of milk, two pounds of flour, teaspoonful of sugar, some salt, large tablespoonful of butter, one of lard. Boil the milk, add the butter and lard; when cool, set a sponge at night; mix the sugar and salt in the flour. In the morning, make a soft dough with the remainder of the flour; make out small cakes by hand, set them to rise again, and bake in a moderately hot oven.

GOOSONG BREAKFAST ROLLS.

Set a sponge over night with a quart and a pint of flour, pint of milk, one cake of compressed yeast, one tablespoonful of butter, one of lard; put the butter and lard in the milk to boil; then, when it has boiled, take it off the range and set it away to cool. Before you make the sponge, dissolve the yeast-cake in luke-warm water; add a little salt and a teaspoonful of sugar. In the morning, make up into small cakes, and put them in a pan to rise; then bake in a brisk oven for fifteen minutes.

PARKER HOUSE ROLLS.

One pint of milk, one cupful of yeast, butter the size of two eggs, one tablespoonful of sugar, one teaspoonful of salt, and two quarts of flour. Let the milk come to a boil, with the butter in it. When tepid, set a batter in the morning; at noon, roll out the thickness of an inch, cut them round, spread butter over them, turn them over half, and bake them about twenty minutes.

GIGGLESWICK DROPPED SCONES.

Take a half-pound of flour, half-ounce of sugar, pinch of salt, two teaspoonfuls of Royal Baking Powder, half-pint of milk. Mix together; grease the griddle with beef suet in a piece of light paper, then drop the scones on. When they are brown, turn them.

MARYLAND BISCUIT.

Take three pints of flour, some salt, three heaping tablespoonfuls of lard; rub the lard all fine in the flour, then pour in enough ice-water to make a stiff dough. Put the dough on the pie-board and beat fully twenty minutes. Then make them out with your hands in little round cakes, about the size of a big walnut, and put them on the greased pans; prick them all over the tops with a fork; put them in a quick oven and bake twenty minutes.

MINNESOTA BISCUIT.

One large cupful of bran flour, one large cupful of wheat flour, one pint of milk, two well beaten eggs, salt. Mix together and bake in small cake shapes, in a quick oven. Indian meal can be used instead of bran flour.

POTATO MUFFINS.

One pound of grated potatoes, two pounds of flour, two ounces of lard, one pint of milk, half-teacupful of yeast; mix together, and set them to rise; then roll out thin and bake.

WAFFLES.

Stir into a quart of flour sufficient luke-warm milk to make a thick batter. The milk should be stirred in gradually, so as to have it free from lumps. Put in a tablespoonful of melted butter. two beaten eggs, a teaspoonful of salt, and a half-teacupful of yeast. When risen, fill your waffle-irons with the batter, and bake them on a bed of coals. When they have been on the fire two or three minutes, turn the waffle-iron over. Serve up with powdered white sugar and cinnamon, if liked.

CATSKILL CORN BREAD.

One quart of milk scalded and thickened with enough Indian meal to make a thin mush; add one teaspoonful of Royal Baking Powder, one tablespoonful of brown sugar and four eggs, well beaten; add enough meal to make as thick as pound-cake; add salt. Bake one hour.

SAUCES.

THE ATTICA APPLE SAUCE.

Pare, core and quarter good baking apples—cider-apples are the best. Put them in a preserving-kettle and cover with water; when they begin to get tender, strew some white sugar over them and let them boil until done, but do not let them break.

THE Y. M. MINT SAUCE.

Two tablespoonfuls of chopped green mint, one tablespoonful of granulated sugar, and a quarter of a pint of vinegar. Pick and wash the green mint very clean, and chop it fine; mix the sugar in a sauce-tureen; put in the mint and let it stand.

CAPER SAUCE.

Take two large tablespoonfuls of capers and a little vinegar; stir them for some time into a half-pint of thick melted butter. This sauce is for boiled mutton.

CURRANT JELLY SAUCE.

Melt together equal parts of currant jelly and butter—or

any rich gravy; season to taste with pepper and salt, and serve hot with cold mutton or venison.

CELERY SAUCE.

Wash a large bunch of celery, and pare it clean; cut it in pieces, and boil it gently in a small quantity of water till it is quite tender; add a little pepper and salt, a piece of butter the size of an egg, rolled in flour, and a half-pint of cream. Boil all together. Celery sauce is eaten with boiled poultry.

QUICK SPANISH SAUCE.

Stir one tablespoonful of butter and one of dry flour over the fire, until they are a light brown in color; then stir gradually into them a pint of boiling water; season the sauce with a teaspoonful of salt and a quarter of a salt-spoonful of pepper; add to it a small onion and a turnip, peeled and sliced very thin, a carrot scraped and sliced thin, a bunch of parsley and sweet herbs. Simmer the sauce slowly for fifteen minutes, and then strain.

BROWN SAUCE.

Put in a saucepan one ounce of butter; when it is very hot, stir into it one ounce of flour. After butter and flour are well mixed, put in half-pint of hot stock, then pepper and salt, one dessert-spoonful of mushroom catsup, one of Worcester Sauce. Let it boil two minutes, then add a few drops of caramel for browning.

PUDDING SAUCE.

Beat up two eggs, two tablespoonfuls of sugar, the juice and grated rind of one lemon. Set it on the fire until it begins to boil; then take it off, add one glass of wine, and serve.

COLD BOSTON SAUCE.

Stir together, as for a pound-cake, equal quantities of fresh butter and powdered white sugar; when quite light and creamy, add some nutmeg and brandy to taste. Send it to table in a glass dish.

WINE SAUCE.

Have ready some rich thick melted or drawn butter, and the moment you take it from the fire, stir in two wine-glassfuls of wine, two tablespoonfuls of sugar and some nutmeg. Serve it with plum-pudding, or any sort of boiled pudding that is made of batter.

ROYAL WINE SAUCE.

Bring slowly to the boiling point half-pint of wine; then add the yolks of four raw eggs and one cupful of white sugar; whip it, on the fire, until it is in a state of high froth and a little thick.

LAKE GEORGE SAUCE.

Take two cupfuls of powdered sugar, one cupful of butter, beaten to a cream. Put in a cupful or more of hot water, and let it come to a boil, stirring all the time; flavor with brandy.

CREAM SAUCE.

Put two-thirds of a pint of cream to boil in a double boiler, to keep it from burning; add some white sugar; then pour it slowly on the beaten whites of two eggs; add one teaspoonful of vanilla.

GERMAN SWEET SAUCE.

One ounce of sugar, two eggs, one wine-glassful of sherry wine. First mix in a saucepan the yolks of the eggs and sugar; then put in the wine, and put it on the cool part of the range, so as to prevent the egg from boiling; then put it in another saucepan over water.

VANILLA SAUCE.

Half-pint of milk in a saucepan on the fire; when scalding hot, add the yolks of three eggs, and stir until as thick as boiled custard; add, when taken from the fire and cooled, a tablespoonful of vanilla and the whites of two eggs, beaten stiff.

THE POTOMAC SAUCE.

Rub to a cream four large spoonfuls of sugar and two of butter. Stir it into a teacupful of hot water. Pour this in a clean saucepan and set it on the fire; stir it steadily until it boils, when add either rose-water or lemon to flavor it. Then give it another quick boil, and grate nutmeg on it.

PASTRY.

GOOD PLAIN PIE-CRUST.

Sift into a pan one pound of the best flour; cut into this a half-pound of hard lard; then moisten it with one pint of ice-water; mix it with a knife. Dust your pie-board well with flour, and turn out your paste; roll out and cut up one-quarter pound of lard and add this in two rollings; handle it as little as possible, and use a knife for mixing the paste; lay it on ice for one hour before baking.

MINCE MEAT.

Take four and a half pounds of beef, two and a half pounds of suet, three pounds of sugar, three pounds of currants, three pounds of raisins, three-quarters of a pound of citron, quarter-pound of candied lemon-peel, half-ounce of cinnamon, quarter-ounce of cloves, quarter-ounce allspice, two grated nutmegs, a few bitter almonds, half-peck of apples, one orange, one quart of cider, one quart of wine, one quart of brandy.

COTTAGE CHEESE CAKE.

One pint of cheese, two eggs, sugar to taste; beat sugar, cheese and one tablespoonful of butter together, with the hand, until light; add half-pint of milk and the eggs when well beaten; flavor with lemon; add one tablespoonful of flour; mix together, and bake in a good crust.

COCOANUT PIE.

Cut off the brown skin of the cocoanut and grate the rest, and simmer the grated cocoanut in a quart of milk for a quarter of an hour; then take it from the fire and mix it with four tablespoonfuls of white sugar, two tablespoonfuls of melted butter, a small cracker rolled fine, half a nutmeg; add, when cold, a wine-glassful of wine, five eggs beaten light. Turn the mixture into plates that have a lining of fine paste, and bake in a quick oven.

CUSTARD PIE.

Take any stale cake, grate it, and mix it as in making cheese cake, using cake instead of cheese. Line a plate with good crust, fill with the custard and bake.

DURENTUM LEMON CUSTARD.

Three cupfuls of sugar, two cupfuls of water, two tablespoonfuls of flour, two large lemons, six eggs beaten light. Mix the flour with the sugar, then add the water, then the grated rind and juice of the lemons. Beat the whites perfectly light; add the yolks to the whites, then add them to the mixture and bake immediately in a crust.

LONG BRANCH LEMON PIE.

Four tablespoonfuls of sugar, four eggs, two-thirds of a cup of flour, nearly a quart of milk, two small lemons, a pinch of salt. Bake two under-crusts; mix the yolks of eggs and sugar well together; bring the milk to the boiling point, then mix the flour with some cold milk quite smooth, and add it to the boiling milk; stir it until it thickens, when remove from the fire; stir in the yolks and sugar, and return it a minute to the fire to set the eggs; again remove it and flavor with lemon-juice and the grated rind. When the crusts are baked pour the mixture over them, then spread the beaten whites, sweetened and flavored; place in the oven a few minutes, to brown.

MOUNTAIN LAKE LEMON PIE.

Grate the rinds of three lemons; two cupfuls of sugar, quarter-pound of butter, one tablespoonful of cracker-dust, six eggs beaten separately. Beat the butter and sugar to a cream; add one cupful of sweet milk, the cracker-dust, the rind of the lemon and the juice; put the whites in last. Bake in a good crust.

MERTON COLLEGE LEMON PIE.

One lemon, one cupful of sugar, one cupful of water, one egg, one tablespoonful of cream, one tablespoonful of flour. Bake in a crust. This will make two pies.

GORDALE LEMON PUDDING.

One pound of sugar, half-pound of butter, five eggs, the rind and juice of two large lemons; add nearly a tumblerful of milk. Beat the sugar and butter to a cream, then add the milk, then the well beaten eggs, then the juice and rind of the lemons, and a wine-glassful of wine or brandy. Bake in a good crust.

MINCE PIES

(MADE FROM REMNANTS OF COLD BEEF).

A good disposition, in winter, of cold roast beef, is to make with it two or three mince pies, as by the following receipt:

One cupful of chopped meat, (quarter of it fat,) two cupfuls of apple, one teaspoonful of salt, one tablespoonful of ground allspice, half-tablespoonful of cinnamon, half-tablespoonful of cloves, one cupful of sugar, half-cupful of raisins, half-cupful of currants, small piece of citron, and candied lemon, one small orange (grated rind and juice), one cupful of cider, half-cupful of wine and brandy, mixed, or more if you like.

VIRGINIA PUMPKIN PIES.

Take the seeds out of a good pumpkin, cut the rind carefully away and then cut the pumpkin into thin and narrow bits. Stew over a moderate fire in a little water (just enough to keep the mass from burning), until soft. Turn off the water, if any remains, and let the pumpkin steam over a slow fire about ten minutes; when sufficiently cool, strain through a sieve. Sweeten the pumpkin with sugar and a little molasses.

The sugar and eggs should be beaten together; the flavoring requires ginger, the grated rind of a lemon, or nutmeg, and salt. To one quart of pumpkin add one quart of milk and four eggs. Heat the pumpkin again scalding hot before putting it upon the crust to bake; otherwise the crust will be soaked. Bake in a very hot oven.

SWEET POTATO PIE.

Three large sweet potatoes, eight well beaten eggs, enough milk to make it quite thin. Mash the potatoes very smooth, then add the milk and eggs, and flavor with vanilla. Bake in a good under-crust.

SCOTCH WHITE POTATO PIE.

Three boiled potatoes, grated, a piece of butter size of an egg, two eggs, one gill of cream, a little nutmeg, two tablespoonfuls of sugar, one tablespoonful of brandy. Beat the sugar and eggs together and mix with the potatoes, then add the rest, except the brandy, which must not be put in until ready to bake. Bake with a good crust.

CALIFORNIA DOUGHNUTS.

Take one pint of boiled milk, one cupful of butter, two cupfuls of sugar, one cupful of mashed potatoes, two eggs, one cupful of yeast, add a little flour. All of these ingredients mix at noon and allow to stand until bed-time; then mix enough flour to make a soft dough. Next morning roll out for baking; the dough should be as soft as can be handled.

PUDDINGS.

APPLE CUSTARD.

Pare, quarter and core six tart apples; set them, with six spoonfuls of water, in a pan on the range, and as they soften, put them in a pudding-dish and sprinkle sugar on; and mix eight eggs, beaten with rolled brown sugar, with three pints of milk; grate in some nutmeg, and turn the whole over the apples. Bake about twenty-five minutes.

APPLE DUMPLINGS.

Wash and boil three white potatoes, and grate them; mix well with enough flour to make ten or twelve dumplings; add water and salt. Roll out the dough, and put an apple in each piece of crust. Place them in nets, and then put them in hot water, and boil half an hour.

BAG PUDDING.

One quart of flour, one tincupful of milk, four eggs, a small teaspoonful of soda. Boil in a tin kettle one hour and a half.

Sauce—one half-pint of milk, one egg, four tablespoonfuls of sugar; let it come to a boil; flavor with wine or lemon.

LENOIR BATTER PUDDING.

One pint of milk, three eggs, pinch of salt, one pint of flour. Mix all well together, and bake half an hour. To be eaten with sauce.

SUET BATTER PUDDING.

Beat eight eggs very light, mix them in a pint of milk, pinch of salt; mix by degrees enough flour to make a pretty stiff batter; then add a quarter-pound of beef suet, half-pound of seeded raisins, three teaspoonfuls of Royal Baking Powder. Grease a shape well, and flour it, then put the batter in and put it in a pot of boiling water; boil for three hours. To be eaten with vanilla sauce.

BERRY PUDDING—Boiled or Steamed.

Take two cupfuls of flour, one cupful of sour milk, two eggs, one teaspoonful of baking powder, quarter of a cupful of molasses, one pint of berries. Cook one hour.

BOILED BREAD PUDDING.

Take half-pound of stale bread-crumbs, half-pound of beef suet, chopped fine, one quart of milk, half-pound of seeded raisins, half-pound of currants, four eggs, teaspoonful of baking powder; add flour to make a stiff batter; put it in a greased mould and boil three hours. Serve with sauce.

"THE ARCADIAN" BREAD PUDDING.

Take light white bread, cut it in thin slices, put it in a pudding-mould and spread on it any kind of preserve, then slices of bread, and repeat until the mould is full. Pour over all a pint of warm milk in which four beaten eggs have been mixed; cover the mould with a piece of linen, then place it in a saucepan containing a little boiling water. Let it boil twenty minutes. Serve with sauce.

BROWN BETTY PUDDING.

Put a layer of apples, chopped fine, in a baking-dish, sprinkle with cinnamon and sugar, a layer of bread-crumbs with butter, cinnamon and sugar, then another layer of apples, and repeat until the dish is filled. Bake it an hour to an hour and a half in a good oven. Make a sauce of one pint of milk, one egg, four tablespoonfuls of sugar; let it come to a boil; flavor with vanilla, lemon, nutmeg or wine, as you please.

BOILED FRUIT PUDDING.

Make a crust as for boiled dumplings; line a bowl, that has a rim round it, with the paste. Then fill it with plums, or gooseberries, with plenty of sugar; put a crust over and trim off the edges and press the edges together. Then put a plate over the bowl, then a pudding-cloth over that; tie it with strong twine; take up the ends of the cloth, and pin it on top, and put it in boiling water. Boil it two hours.

ORCHARD CHERRY PUDDING.

Make a batter of one pint of milk, three eggs, teaspoonful of baking powder, a pinch of salt, with flour enough to make a stiff batter. Have ready two quarts of sour cherries, seeded; mix them in the batter. Put the pudding in a floured bag or mould, and boil one hour and a half. To be eaten with strawberry-sauce, made of one quart of strawberries, mashed, half-cupful of butter, one and a half cupfuls of sugar; mix the butter and sugar to a cream; add the berries and serve.

COLD CHOCOLATE PUDDING.

Take a quarter-pound of chocolate, one pint of milk, the yolks of four eggs, a teaspoonful of vanilla, one ounce of sugar, half-ounce of gelatine, and a half-gill of cold water; grate the chocolate and put it in the milk to boil with the water; melt the gelatine. When the chocolate and milk boil, draw them aside to cool a little, then put the eggs in a basin and pour the milk and chocolate over them; then add the sugar and melted gelatine. Pour all this back into the saucepan, and stir all the ingredients over the fire until the eggs set. Then add the vanilla, which should be the last thing of all; put it in a mould to cool. Serve with cream.

COTTAGE PUDDING.

Beat to a cream one cupful of good brown sugar, and two and a half large spoonfuls of good butter. When well creamed, stir in two well-whipped eggs, a little grated nutmeg, and a large spoonful of orange-flower water; sift into a pan one pint of flour; add two teaspoonfuls of Royal Baking Powder. Mix the flour and eggs and spice together, then add the milk; beat these well together; butter a baking-dish and pour in the pudding. Bake half an hour, and serve with wine sauce.

DANDY PUDDING.

Take six eggs, two quarts of milk; separate the yolks, and add two tablespoonfuls of flour; make it like soft custard; beat the whites to a froth, with sugar to make it thick enough to drop on the custard; put it in the pudding-dish, and brown it in the oven.

ENGLISH PLUM PUDDING.

Take one pound of raisins, one pound and a quarter of flour, three-quarters of a pound of suet, one pound of currants, half-pound of sugar, six eggs, half of a nutmeg, one teaspoonful of cinnamon, half-pint of milk, one ounce of candied lemon, half-ounce of citron, salt-spoonful of salt, two teaspoonfuls of baking powder, six bitter almonds or a small teaspoonful of extract of almonds, one wine-glassful of brandy. Mix the flour and milk together, then add the eggs well beaten, then the fruit, (the raisins being stoned); beat all well, as much depends on the stirring. Add the spice and brandy; then grease and flour a tin mould, put the batter into it, and place the mould in a pot of boiling water; don't let the water come to the top of the mould. Boil it six hours.

In chopping suet, sprinkle flour over it while chopping, to prevent the pieces from adhering.

FIG PUDDING.

Take three-quarters of a pound of grated bread, half-pound of figs, six ounces of suet, teacupful of sugar, a teacupful of milk, and a little nutmeg, the figs and suet to be chopped very fine; mix the bread and suet first, then the figs, sugar, and nutmeg, one egg, and lastly the milk. Boil in a mould four hours. Serve with sauce.

GEORGETOWN CHOCOLATE PUDDING.

Ten tablespoonfuls of grated bread, eight tablespoonfuls of chocolate, one quart of milk, sweetened, and all boiled together until smooth. Add to this the yolks of six eggs and the whites of two. Put in a pudding dish and bake until done (three-quarters of an hour or more). Turn out when cold, and ice with the remaining whites of eggs and three-quarters of a pound of powdered sugar, and one teaspoonful of cream tartar.

INDIAN PUDDING.

Scald two teacupfuls of corn meal with three pints of milk, till as thick as gruel, and when cool, add some ginger, cinnamon, nutmeg, salt, and sugar to suit the taste; add some beef suet, chopped fine, or pieces of butter, some stoned raisins, or fine cut apples. Butter a deep dish and bake one hour.

LINCOLN PUDDING.

Take one pound of lady-fingers, four eggs, split the lady-fingers open and lay jelly over them, as many as will cover a large dinner-plate; lay them across each other, and then whip the whites of the eggs and lay on the top; stand the plate nearly upright before a clear fire to brown. Take the yolks and make a sauce for it.

ORANGE PUDDING.

Grate three sponge biscuits in enough milk to make a paste, beat eight eggs and stir in with the juice of one lemon and half the peel grated. Put in a teacupful of orange juice and one of sugar, with half a cupful of melted butter in the mixture—stir it well, put it in a dish with puff-paste around it, and bake slowly one hour.

ORANGE CUSTARD PUDDING.

Slice thin six oranges and put in a pudding-dish, throwing over them three-quarters of a cupful of sugar. Make a soft custard of a pint of milk, three eggs, omitting the whites, and one-half a cupful of sugar, then beat the whites of the eggs very light, adding a little powdered sugar, put them over the top and brown. This can be baked in a good crust.

QUEEN PUDDING.

Three eggs, pint of milk, half-pint of bread-crumbs, half lemon rind, grated, two teacupfuls of white sugar. Beat the whites separately, bake the pudding; then let it get cold, put on fruit of any kind. Then put the beaten whites of eggs on top.

"TALLYHO" RICE PUDDING.

Take one teacupful of boiled rice, one pint of milk, the yolks of five eggs, and the rind of one lemon, grated. Mix together and bake it; then beat the whites, with one pound of sugar, powdered, and spread over the top, when the pudding is baked. Then put it in the oven to brown it.

PLAIN RICE PUDDING.

To two quarts of milk, put a small teacupful of washed rice, three tablespoonfuls of sugar, teaspoonful of extract of almond, a small piece of butter, some cinnamon or nutmeg. Bake until the rice is soft.

ROLLY POLLY.

Make a crust of one pound of flour, a large tablespoonful of lard, enough ice-water to make a dough; roll out in a sheet, and spread preserves on and roll up; press the ends well together, so that the juice won't run out; then roll up in a pudding cloth carefully tie or pin it, and put this in a pot of boiling water, and boil one hour. Serve with or without sauce.

SNOW PUDDING.

Put some water on some gelatine and let it stand; then take the whites of eggs and beat light; then add them to the gelatine; beat well; then put it in a form. Eat with a sauce of soft custard, flavored with lemon.

ST. AUGUSTINE ORANGE PUDDING.

Make a soft custard with one pint of milk, the yolks of two eggs, two tablespoonfuls of sugar, one teaspoonful of corn-starch; flavor with the grated rind of two oranges. Line a pudding-dish with a good crust, slice two oranges, put them on the crust, then turn the custard over the oranges and bake ten or fifteen minutes; beat the whites of the two eggs and a tablespoonful of powdered sugar, spread it over the top when the pudding is baked; put it again in the oven to brown slightly. To be eaten with any kind of sauce. Any kind of fruit may be used.

SUET PUDDING.

Take half-pound of suet, chopped fine, half-pound of sugar, half-pound of bread, the rind of two lemons, the yolks of four eggs, white of one; butter the basin, lay a few raisins at the bottom; put the mixture in, put a paper over the top, and steam three hours.

FRUIT TAPIOCA PUDDING.

Soak four tablespoonfuls of tapioca in a quart of water for an hour; pare and slice, or quarter some baking apples; put them in a baking-dish with three tablespoonfuls of sugar; pour the tapioca over the apples and bake until it is clear and the apples soft. When cold, serve with cream.

VIENNESE PUDDING.

Five ounces bread-crumbs, one ounce lump-sugar, three ounces soft sugar, three ounces Sultana raisins, two ounces of candied peel, one glass of sherry, half-pint of milk, yolks of four eggs, one teaspoonful of vanilla. Put the lump-sugar in a small dry saucepan; when it melts and browns, add to it the milk, and stir well until the milk becomes brown; cut the bread in small square pieces, and put them in a basin; rub the raisins in a dry towel, then add them to the bread; add also the peel (cut in very small pieces), and the soft sugar; pour over all these dry ingredients a glass of sherry; put in a separate basin the yolks of the four eggs, mix them slightly, and pour over them, through a strainer, the colored milk; mix all the ingredients together, and add last the vanilla. Grease well a mould, and put the mixture in, twist over the top a piece of paper, and steam an hour and a half.

D.

VERMICELLI PUDDING.

Wash quarter-pound of vermicelli, boil it a quarter of an hour in a pint of milk with a piece of cinnamon and lemon-peel; when done take off the fire, and when nearly cold take out the cinnamon and peel. Sweeten to taste, and add the yolks of six eggs, and the whites of two; mix and bake in a buttered dish half an hour. Or it may be boiled for one and a half hours, and served with sauce.

DISHES FOR DESSERT.

CREAM FOR FILLING CAKES.

Half-cupful of flour, one cupful of sugar, two eggs. Boil one pint of new milk; beat the flour, eggs and sugar together, and stir into the milk while boiling, until sufficiently scalded. Flavor with extract of vanilla or lemon. Boil the milk in a farina boiler.

LEMON CONSERVE.

Take six eggs, quarter-pound of butter, one pound of sugar, the juice and rind of three lemons. Beat the eggs light and add the lemons; put them in a pan with the sugar on the range, and stir in the butter; keep stirring it all the time, about ten minutes.

MACAROON CUSTARD.

TIME—HALF-HOUR.

They should be made in custard-cups. Put a macaroon in the bottom of each cup, and pour on it a tablespoonful of wine; mix together a pint of cream and a pint of milk, and boil them with a stick of cinnamon, broken up, or a teaspoonful of extract of almonds. Then strain the milk, stir in a quarter-pound of white sugar and set it away to cool; beat light eight eggs (omitting the whites of four), and stir them into the cream and milk when quite cold; fill the cups with the mixture, leaving the macaroons in the cups, and set them in a baking-pan half full of boiling water, and bake the custards ten minutes. When cold, heap the beaten whites of eggs and powdered sugar on the top of each.

ORANGE SOUFFLÉ.

Pare and slice a half-dozen sweet oranges, sugar them well, and let them stand until ready for use. Make a rich custard of the yolks of three eggs, one tablespoonful of corn-starch, one pint of milk, two tablespoonfuls of sugar. Beat the whites of the eggs to a stiff froth, with sufficient powdered sugar to sweeten. Lay sponge-cake or lady-fingers in a glass dish, then spread the oranges on them, then the custard, and lastly the whites of the eggs.

PANCAKES.

One half-pound of flour, one ounce of sugar, two eggs, one-half of a lemon, one-half pint of milk, pinch of salt. Put the flour in a bowl, add yolks of eggs, mix and add one half-pint of milk by degrees; beat well together; beat the whites of eggs very stiff; add a little salt, and then add the whites to the mixture. Melt a little butter in an omelette-pan, drop in half a teacupful of the mixture. When done, turn out on a plate, sprinkle sugar and juice of lemon, and roll up.

D.

POP-OVERS.

Two cupfuls of milk, two cupfuls of flour, two eggs, and an even teaspoonful of salt. Beat the eggs separately—add the whites last—and beat all well together. They may be baked in roll-pans, or deep "Gem" pans, which should be heated and greased before the batter is put in; they should be half filled. Or they may be baked in teacups, of which eight will be required for the quantity of batter; then bake immediately.

RICE MERINGUES.

One teacupful of rice, boiled. When cold, add one quart of milk, the yolks of three eggs, three tablespoonfuls of sugar, a little nutmeg; pour in a dish and bake half an hour. When partly baked, stir a few large raisins through it. When cold, beat the whites with two tablespoonfuls of sugar, and spread over the top; put again in the oven to brown.

FLOATING ISLAND.

Separate the whites of six eggs very carefully from the yolks, and put the yolks on one side; whisk the whites to a stiff froth. Take six tablespoonfuls of jelly and eight tablespoonfuls of powdered sugar, and beat them in the eggs gradually; when it is stiff, pile it up in a china or glass bowl, on some cream, or on a custard made of the yolks of the eggs.

SPANISH CREAM.

One box and one ounce of Cooper's Gelatine, three pints of milk, six eggs, eight tablespoonfuls of white sugar. Put the gelatine in with the milk, and let it soak while the yolks and sugar are being beaten. Put the yolks and sugar in with the milk and gelatine; place on the fire and let it simmer, (not boil,) until the gelatine is thoroughly dissolved. After beating the whites very stiff, pour the above on the whites, beating very hard; then add the juice and rinds of three lemons, or flavor with vanilla. Pour into a mould, and set it near ice, to get cold.

CHESTNUT HILL STRAWBERRY CAKE.

One quart of flour, one teaspoonful of salt, two teaspoonfuls of Royal Baking Powder, two tablespoonfuls of butter, one pint of milk. Sift the flour, salt and powder together, and rub in the butter, cold; add the milk, and mix into a smooth dough just soft enough to handle; divide in half and roll out to the size of breakfast plates; lay on a greased baking-tin, and bake in hot oven twenty minutes; then endeavor, if possible, to separate the cake without cutting, as cutting makes them heavy. Have ready two quarts of berries, use half of them to cover the bottom halves of the cake; sprinkle plentifully with sugar; lay on the top the other halves with the crust downwards, use the rest of the fruit over them, and sugar plentifully.

STRAWBERRY SHORTCAKE.

Make good pie-crust (not biscuit-crust) enough for three layers, rolled a little thicker than for pies, and bake in jelly-cake pans; prepare two quarts of berries, and stir in sugar to taste, about half an hour before the crust is baked; butter the crust while hot, spread the berries between the layers, and serve immediately. No sauce is needed, as the juice of the fruit is sufficient.

STRAWBERRY SPONGE-CAKE.

The yolks of four eggs, one cupful of sugar, one cupful of milk, two tablespoonfuls of butter, teaspoonful of Royal Baking Powder, flour enough to make a batter softer than pound-cake batter; flavor with lemon. Bake in two shallow pans; when done, spread the berries on one, then the beaten whites of the four eggs, beaten light with powdered sugar. Place the other cake over this, then more berries and the whites of eggs on top; place in the oven to brown, or not, as you like.

TAPIOCA CREAM.

Take two tablespoonfuls of tapioca, one and a half pints of milk, four eggs. Boil the milk and tapioca, then beat the yolks of the eggs in; flavor with vanilla, and beat the whites, put them on the top, and put in the oven a few minutes to brown.

VELVET CREAM.

Put three-quarters of a box of Cox's Gelatine in a bowl, and pour over it a cup and a half of wine. Add the rind and juice of one lemon, and let it stand for an hour. Then add three-quarters of a pound of white sugar. Put it over the fire and stir until the sugar is dissolved. Strain, and when cool, pour in a quart of cream, beating hard while pouring in; when about as thick as soft custard pour it into a mould, and set it away to get cold.

BISQUE ICE-CREAM.

Take one quart and one pint of cream, one pint of milk, one quarter of a pound of macaroons, crisped in the oven and then rolled, two teacupfuls of sugar, and half-teacupful of wine. Mix together and freeze.

PEACH ICE-CREAM.

Quarter-peck of ripe peaches, three pints of milk and cream mixed, twenty tablespoonfuls of sugar; mix all together and freeze as ice-cream.

ORANGE WATER-ICE.

Two to four oranges, according to size, to each quart of water one pound of sugar; grate the rind of one orange and one lemon, and freeze.

LEMON WATER-ICE.

The juice of four lemons, the rind of one, one quart of cold water, one pound of sugar.

Strawberry Ice.

One quart of strawberries to two quarts of water, and two pounds of sugar.

Pine Apple.

One pine-apple to two quarts of water, one pound of sugar to each quart of water.

Roman Punch.

The same as Orange Water-Ice, and add good brandy or Jamaica rum.

FROZEN CUSTARD.

Three pints of cream, one quart of milk, eight eggs, eighteen tablespoonfuls of sifted sugar, one tablespoonful of extract of vanilla. Put the milk and cream on the fire, and when it boils add the eggs well beaten and mixed with the sugar. Let all boil about five minutes; add the vanilla after you take the custard from the fire. This will make sufficient for twelve persons. Freeze as ice-cream.

FROZEN PEACHES.

One quart of cream, half-pound of sugar, quarter-peck of good peaches, or two cans of peaches. Mash all as fine as possible, and freeze as ice-cream.

PLAIN SWEET CAKES.

ALBANY CAKES.

Take one pound of butter (best to have it a little softened, not melted), two pounds of brown sugar, six eggs, thirty drops of oil of lemon, one teaspoonful of soda, or two teaspoonfuls of Royal Baking Powder, three pounds of flour. Mix some sugar with the flour to roll out with, cut with a cutter and bake.

COCOANUT SPONGE CAKE.

Two cupfuls of sugar, three cupfuls of flour, one cupful of milk, three eggs, butter the size of an egg, two teaspoonfuls of baking powder, one cocoanut, grated. Bake in jelly cake pans. This makes six cakes; put the icing on one cake, then sprinkle the cocoanut on, then another cake, and so on until you have three layers. The six will make two cakes when done. The icing is made of the whites of three eggs and two cupfuls of powdered sugar.

COMPOSITION CAKE.

One and three-quarters of a pound of flour, half-pound of butter, one and a quarter pounds of sugar, four eggs, one nutmeg, one teacupful of milk, three-quarters of a pound of raisins, three-quarters of a pound of currants, two teaspoonfuls of baking powder. Beat the butter and sugar very light, add by degrees the milk and quarter of the flour; beat the eggs until thick; mix the baking powder in the flour and add it to the batter; beat well and add spice and the fruit.

CRULLERS.

Take one pint of milk, half-pound of white sugar, quarter-pound of butter, beaten to a cream; add three eggs, half-teaspoonful of cinnamon, half of a nutmeg, two pounds of flour, two teaspoonfuls of baking powder, put in after all is mixed. Roll out and cut in small cakes; fry in plenty of sweet lard.

FRANKLIN BUNS.

Six ounces of butter, three-quarters of a pound of sugar, half a pound of flour, one of cream, three eggs, one wineglassful of rose water, one wineglassful of wine, the grating of one nutmeg, teaspoonful of baking powder. Beat the butter and sugar until light, stir in the cream gradually with half the flour, then whisk the eggs until thick, and add them with the remaining flour, half at a time; beat well. Then add the other engredients; after beating all well together, butter a square pan, put in the mixture and bake in a moderate oven. When done, sift white sugar and cut in squares.

FRUIT CAKE.

One pound of butter, one pound of sugar, one pound of flour, twelve eggs, two tablespoonfuls of mace, one tablespoonful of cinnamon, four nutmegs, one teaspoonful of cloves, two pounds of currants, two pounds of raisins, one pound of citron, one tumblerful of brandy, put in last. Bake six hours.

HARD GINGERBREAD.

Take two pounds of flour, quarter pound of lard, quarter pound of butter, quarter pound of sugar, four tablespoonfuls of ginger, two tablespoonfuls of cinnamon, one of cloves and allspice mixed, one teaspoonful of soda; rub the shortening in the flour, then add the spices and sugar; dissolve the soda in a little milk and add molasses enough to make a dough. Let it stand two hours in a cool place, then roll out very thin and bake.

SOFT GINGERBREAD.

Take one cupful of molasses, one cupful of sugar, half-cupful of butter and lard mixed, one cupful of sour milk, two eggs, three cupfuls of flour, two teaspoonfuls of soda, two teaspoonfuls of cinnamon, one and a half of cloves, a little grated nutmeg. Bake in square tins fifteen or twenty minutes.

SOUTHERN SOFT GINGERBREAD.

Three teacupfuls of flour, one of butter, two of molasses, one tablespoonful of ginger, and half a nutmeg, teaspoonful of cinnamon, and three eggs, beat them all up together till they are light; dissolve half a teaspoonful of baking soda in a little hot water, while you stir about three-quarters of a cupful of hot water into the cake; when it is well stirred put in the soda and mix it in well. Pour into well greased baking-tins and put in the oven; watch carefully, as it is apt to burn.

JINGO GINGER-NUTS.

One quart of molasses, one pound of sugar, half-pound of butter, half-pound of lard, quarter-pound of ginger, one tablespoonful of allspice and cloves mixed, two tablespoonfuls of cinnamon, spoonful of soda, and as much flour as will roll them out not too stiff.

SHINY BACKS.

One quart of molasses, one cupful of lard, two eggs, two cupfuls of sugar, half pint of sour milk, one large tablespoonful of saleratus, two tablespoonfuls of ginger, and cinnamon if you like; use as little flour as possible; roll out, cut into cakes, and bake in a quick oven.

LADY CAKE.

One cupful of butter, two cupfuls of sugar, three of flour, one of milk, two teaspoonfuls of baking powder, one teaspoonful of almond flavoring, and the whites of eight eggs. Bake in a square pan.

MARBLE CAKE.

BLACK CAKE.—One cupful of brown sugar, half-cupful of molasses, half-cupful of butter, half-cupful of buttermilk, two cupfuls of flour, yolks of four eggs, one teaspoonful of Royal

Baking Powder, one teaspoonful of cinnamon, cloves, allspice and nutmeg mixed.

WHITE CAKE.—The whites of four eggs, half-cupful of butter, half-cupful of buttermilk, two cupfuls of flour, two of sugar, one teaspoonful of baking powder.

Put a layer of white, then a layer of black cake, alternately, and bake.

MARY'S CAKE.

Three cupfuls of flour, three eggs, one cupful of milk, quarter-pound of butter, one and a half cupfuls of sugar, two teaspoonfuls of Royal Baking Powder, rubbed dry in the flour; flavor with extract of almond. Beat sugar and butter to a cream, then add the eggs, then flour, then milk; put the mixture in buttered cake-pan and bake in a moderate oven. Make an icing of the whites of two well beaten eggs, enough powdered sugar to stiffen it. Spread on the cake while hot.

ORANGE CAKE.

Grate the rind of half an orange, half-cupful of butter, one cupful of sugar, two eggs, one teacupful of milk, one tincupful of flour, teaspoonful and a half of baking powder, sift with the flour, and mix all together; bake in a long pan in a quick oven. Make an icing of the white of one egg, one and a half teacupfuls of pulverized sugar, and the juice of half an orange.

POUND CAKE.

Sift one pound of the finest flour; beat to a cream one pound of butter and one pound of white sugar; when they are perfectly light, beat ten eggs light, and add by degrees, into the mixture, alternately with the flour; then add one teaspoonful of extract of lemon, one small glassful of wine, and one of brandy. Beat all well together, and put it in a deep tin pan, with upright or straight sides. Bake in a moderate oven from two to three hours. Ice it.

KALOOLA CAKE.

Half pound of sugar, one lemon, quarter-pound of butter, one pound of flour, two teacupfuls of milk, one teaspoonful of baking powder. Mix well and bake in a quick oven, or bake it in pie-plates, and fill it with preserves. This makes a very good pie for dyspeptics.

SNOWFLAKE CAKE.

Take a half-cupful of butter, three eggs, two cupfuls of sugar, four of flour, one of milk, two teaspoonfuls of Royal Baking Powder. Stir butter and sugar together, add the beaten yolks and half the flour, with the baking powder in it; pour in the milk, beat the whites and mix in; then stir in the rest of the flour. Bake in jelly-cake tins. Grate two cocoanuts, add to them one cup of sugar and the beaten whites of two eggs; spread between the cakes, and heap the cocoanut on top.

SPONGE CAKE.

One pound of sugar, half pound of flour, two eggs, two lemons; mix the sugar and yolks together, then add the grated rind and juice of the lemons, the whites of the eggs beaten stiff; add the flour very slowly; butter a Turk's turban and bake.

WEST END SPONGE CAKE.

Four eggs beaten light, then add one cupful of sugar, and one of sifted flour; one lemon to flavor.

CREAM SPONGE CAKE.

Beat three eggs two minutes, add one and a half cupfuls of white sugar, and beat five minutes; then one cupful of flour, and beat one minute; add half-cupful of cold water; flavor with lemon or vanilla; add one heaping teaspoonful of baking powder, a little pinch of salt. Bake in jelly-cake pans—make two layers or cakes—one grated cocoanut.

CREAM FOR FILLING.—The yolks of two eggs, one cupful of sugar, half-teacupful of corn-starch, half-pint of milk, one teaspoonful of lemon; make into a custard; when nearly cold spread on the cake, which must be quite cold; sprinkle some grated cocoanut on the cream. For the top layer make an icing of the whites of two eggs and a half pound of sugar, powdered, and spread on the top and sprinkle cocoanut over all.

WALNUT CAKE.

One cupful of milk, three-quarters of a cupful of butter, two cupfuls of granulated sugar, three cupfuls of flour, three eggs, three teaspoonfuls of baking powder, not quite a cupful of English Walnuts, broken up. Bake in two square pans or tins. Frost both cakes with icing; put one on top of the other; divide the icing into small squares, laying half a nut in each square. For icing, use whites of two eggs and one half-pound of pulverized sugar. One pound of walnuts is required for this cake.

WASHINGTON CAKE.

Three cupfuls of sugar, one cupful of butter, beaten to a cream; then add one cupful of cream, five eggs, four cupfuls of flour, two teaspoonfuls of baking powder. Bake in jelly-cake pans, with cream between.

WHITE CAKE.

Three cupfuls of sifted flour, one and a half cupfuls of sugar, one egg, one teacupful of sweet milk, two tablespoonfuls of butter, teaspoonful of baking powder, and one teaspoonful of vanilla, almond, or lemon essence. Beat the butter and sugar to a cream; mix the baking powder in the flour, add the milk with the eggs, well beaten, to the butter and sugar, and the essence; mix with this, very slowly, the flour, and when well incorporated, bake in a quick oven.

FANCY CAKES.

ANGELS' FOOD.

Take two and a half gills of flour, three and three-quarters gills of sugar, whites of eleven eggs, one teaspoonful of vanilla. Sift the flour before you measure it; after measuring it, sift four times; then put one teaspoonful of cream of tartar in the flour, and sift again. Beat the whites of the eggs to a stiff froth, then stir in the sugar, then the flour, and then the flavor. Bake in a pan, not greased, forty minutes. When done, turn the pan upside down until perfectly cold. Ice it all over.

CHOCOLATE JUMBLES.

Take one pound of sugar, half-pound of chocolate, grated, whites of eight eggs or four whole eggs, well beaten, six ounces of flour, one teaspoonful of cinnamon, one-half teaspoonful of cloves. Line the pans with white paper, buttered, and drop the mixture on with a teaspoon. Some think it an improvement to add a pint of broken nuts and mix in it.

COCOANUT BALLS.

Two grated cocoanuts, half-pound of sugar, the whites of three eggs. Mix all together; make in balls, and bake a few minutes in a quick oven.

COCOANUT DROP-CAKE.

One-half pound of butter, two cupfuls of sugar, four of flour, one cocoanut, four eggs, one heaping teaspoonful of baking powder, one teaspoonful of lemon; mix all together, and drop on tins and bake in a quick oven. Take care they don't burn.

PENNYGHENT JUMBLES.

Rub into one pound and a half of flour one pound of butter; beat five eggs light, then lightly put them in with your hand, along with one pound of sugar. Let them stand an hour or two to stiffen; roll and make them up with sugar and flour. Bake in a slow oven.

NO NAME CAKES.

One and a half cupfuls of sifted sugar, half cupful of cream, six eggs, two pinches of salt, piece of butter the size of a walnut; add flour enough to roll out, cut any shape to suit yourself; roll them very thin, and cook in lard.

NUT KISSES.

One pint of walnuts, whites of two eggs, one pound of pulverized sugar. Beat the whites stiff, then beat in the sugar, then stir in slowly the walnuts; line the pans with paper, drop in the mixture, and bake in a quick oven.

ICING.

Half a teacupful of water, three teacupfuls of sugar, and the whites of three eggs. Boil the sugar and water until quite thick, pour it on the whites of the eggs, previously beaten light, and beat all together until cool.

BOILED ICING.

Ingredients:—One pound of sugar and the whites of three eggs.

First boil the sugar with a little water; when it is ready to candy, or will spin in threads when dropping from the end of a spoon, take it off the fire, and while it is boiling hot add the whites of three eggs, well beaten, stirring them in as fast as possible. Flavor with lemon or vanilla, and it is ready for use. Spread it over the cake as soon as taken from the oven. The icing made with the white of one egg is quite sufficient to frost an ordinary sized cake.

PRESERVES,

JELLIES, BEVERAGES, CANDIES, ETC.

APPLES PRESERVED LIKE GINGER.

Peel and cut in quarters six pounds of apples, six pounds of sugar, one-half pound of raw ginger. Pack the apples in a jar, a layer of apples, then sugar and ginger, and so on until all are put in. Next day bruise one ounce of ginger and infuse it in a half-pint of boiling water, closely covered. The day following put the apples, ginger, sugar, and the water from the bruised ginger, in a kettle and boil one hour, or until the apples look clear, and syrup rich. Add some lemon peel cut very thin just before the apples are done.

TO PRESERVE GREEN GAGES.

Choose the finest green gages, stick them with a needle all over; take out the seeds and weigh and place on dishes the hollow side up; have ready an equal weight of granulated sugar, and strew it over them. When the fruit has lain twelve hours put it in a preserving kettle, and let it simmer until the pieces are quite clear, being careful to take off the skum as it rises. Large blue plums may be preserved in the same way.

PRESERVED QUINCES.

No. 1.—Allow three-quarters of a pound of sugar to one pound of quinces. Pare, core, and quarter the quinces; boil them in just enough water to cover them; when tender take them out very carefully, and put them on a dish; then make a syrup of one pint of the water the quinces were boiled in to two pounds of the sugar; when it is clear and boiling hot, add the quinces, and boil until you can run a broom straw easily through them; then put them in glass jars, and seal up with paper and the white of egg.

No. 2.—To two pounds of fruit, put a half-pound of sugar, and four teacupfuls of water, and cook until they turn red.

Jelly.—The parings and cores boil up and strain through a jelly bag, and allow one pound of sugar to one pint of juice, and boil until it jellies.

TO PRESERVE STRAWBERRIES WHOLE.

Choose the largest scarlet strawberries, not too ripe. For every pound of fruit allow three-quarters of a pound of white sugar, pulverized; spread the fruit on large dishes, and sprinkle over it half the sugar; shake the dish gently, so that the sugar may come in contact with the under side of the fruit. On the following day make a thin syrup with the remaining half of the sugar, and pour the juice from the berries on the sugar, and in this syrup simmer the strawberries until sufficiently jellied. When done place them in glass jars or tumblers; when cold, cover with brandied paper, and paste paper over each, with the white of egg.

PRESERVED TOMATOES.

Select the small yellow tomatoes, take a few at a time, scald them just enough to loosen the skins, peel them and allow one pound of granulated sugar to each pound of fruit; prepare a syrup, and then put the tomatoes and the peel of a large lemon into it. Let them simmer a few minutes, then add the juice of the lemon; when the tomatoes appear clear and soft, take them out of the syrup, one at a time; put them in tumblers or small jars; pour the syrup over them warm. When cold cover them with brandied paper, and paste paper over them.

ORANGE MARMALADE.

Take large fine oranges with thin dark-colored skins. Weigh them and allow to each pound of oranges one pound of sifted sugar; pare off the yellow outside rind from half of the oranges as thin as possible, put these rinds in a pan with plenty of cold water, cover it closely, and boil slowly till they are so soft that the head of a pin will pierce them. In the meantime grate the rind from the remainder of the oranges, and put the rind aside; quarter the oranges and take out all the pulp, removing the seeds and core. Put the sugar in the preserving-kettle with a half-pint of water to each pound of fruit; when the sugar is all dissolved, put the kettle on the fire and boil and skim till the syrup is quite clear and thick. Next take the boiled parings, cut them in small pieces, half an inch long; put them in the sugar and boil ten minutes. Then put in the pulp and juice, and the grated rind; boil together twenty minutes, till a transparent mass is formed. When cold put in glass jars, laying brandied paper on top.

Lemon marmalade can be made in the same way, using a pound and a half of sugar.

SPICED PEACHES.

To seven pounds of pared peaches use four pounds of sugar, half-pint of vinegar, spices to taste. Make the syrup, and when warm put the peaches in it and let them simmer, and then take them out. Next day repeat.

SPICED PLUMS.

Five quarts or seven pounds of blue plums, three pounds of sugar, one quart of vinegar, one ounce of whole cloves, and a stick of cinnamon. Put all together in a preserving kettle and boil until done.

BRANDIED PEACHES.

Scald smoothly pared peaches in an ordinary syrup, until soft enough to run a straw in; place them in a jar; make a fresh rich syrup; to one pint of syrup add one pint and a half of the best whisky or brandy. Pour this over the peaches and let it stand over night; if the syrup looks thin, boil it over again and add more sugar.

BOULEVARD BRANDIED PEACHES.

Half-gallon of peach brandy, four pounds of sugar, and eight pounds of peaches. Dissolve the sugar in the brandy.

Boil the peaches in clear water until you can run a straw through them easily; then drop them into the brandy while hot. Do not cook the brandy, the fruit will cook it enough. Seal up at once.

CURRANT JELLY.

Wash, but do not stem the currants, mash them and strain through a jelly strainer. Take a pound of sugar for each pint of juice, and put the juice in the preserving-kettle and put it on the range alone. When it begins to boil, stir the sugar in gradually; let it boil, after all the sugar is in, five minutes; take it from the fire and fill tumblers, and paste white paper, with whites of eggs, over them.

GELATINE JELLY.

On one box of gelatine pour one pint of cold water; on two pounds of white sugar pour three pints of boiling water; grate the rind of three lemons in the syrup, and add the juice. Let the gelatine stand for a half-hour, then pour it on the sugar and water, add a pint of wine; then strain it through book muslin.

ORANGE JELLY.

Whites of two eggs, eight sweet oranges, two lemons, quarter-pound of sugar, one ounce of gelatine, and one gill of cold water; grate the rinds of the oranges and lemons; melt the sugar in a small saucepan with half-gill of water; when melted add the juice and rind of the oranges and lemons.

Soak the gelatine for ten minutes with half a gill of cold water; then add to the other ingredients. Whip the eggs slightly and pour them into the saucepan; whisk all together until it boils; then put on the lid of the saucepan and allow it to simmer for twenty minutes. Pour through a flannel bag, and then pour it in the mould. D.

WINE WHEY.

Boil a pint of new milk, sweeten to taste, and throw in a wine-glassful of sherry. As soon as the curd forms, strain the whey through muslin.

GINGER BEER.

On three pounds of brown sugar, two and a half tablespoonfuls of the best ginger, and two fresh lemons, thinly sliced, pour two gallons of boiling water, and stir in two teaspoonfuls of cream-tartar; mix all well together; when cool strain, and when quite cold add one pint of yeast, then bottle and cork tight, and in twenty-four hours it is fit for use.

RASPBERRY SYRUP.

Wash berries and strain them the same as for jelly. Then for every quart of juice put one pound of white sugar and boil the whole about half an hour until it becomes slightly thick. Bottle it while hot.

CHOCOLATE CARAMELS.

Put half a cake of chocolate in a porcelain kettle, then add two cupfuls of sugar, a half-cupful of New Orleans molasses, one cupful of good sweet milk, and a quarter of a pound of butter; then put the kettle on the range to boil; put a little to cool on a plate; if it is stiff, then stir in two tablespoonfuls of vanilla, then pour the whole into flat greased pans. When the caramels are getting cold take a knife and mark them in squares.

DOMESTIC CONFECTION.

"The peel of the orange preserved in sugar is one of the most delightful confections which a family can use. The peel should of course be clean, and should be cut in long strips and thin. Stew it in water till all the bitterness is extracted. Throw away the water and stew again for half an hour in a thick syrup, made of a pound of sugar to one pound of peel, with just water enough. Put away in a cool place for flavoring puddings, pies, etc. For this purpose it should be chopped very fine."

PICKLES.

CHOW-CHOW.

Take four stalks of celery, one pint of small onions, three large cauliflowers, twelve large pickles, cut up small, or twenty-five very small ones, as you prefer, quarter-pound of mustard, five cents worth of tumeric; put all these in an earthen pan, and salt them and let them stand for twelve hours. Boil three quarts of the best cider vinegar ten minutes; take the pickles out of the salt and throw the vinegar on them. Fill your jars, and seal them up.

COLD TOMATO CATSUP.

Chop fine half-peck of ripe tomatoes, two grated roots of horseradish, two red peppers (without the seeds), one teacupful of black and white mustard-seed, one teacupful of salt, one teacupful of white sugar, two teaspoonfuls of black pepper, one teaspoonful of powdered cloves, one teaspoonful of powdered mace, one teaspoonful of cinnamon, one quart of vinegar, two or three stalks of celery.

GREEN TOMATO PICKLES.

Wash and slice half-bushel of green tomatoes, also a dozen onions and a few blades of garlic, twelve pods of green peppers—all sliced; sprinkle salt over them, and let them lie all night; in the morning drain them; put two ounces of mixed mustard, two ounces of raw ginger, two ounces of allspice, one ounce of mace, and one ounce of tumeric in a muslin bag; all the spices must be ground and mixed together; put a layer of tomatoes and spices alternately in the kettle; add strong vinegar, two gallons to this quantity, and two pounds of brown sugar. Boil until they are tender.

PEPPER SAUCE.

Six large heads of cabbage, one dozen and a half of green peppers, four tablespoonfuls of celery-seed, four of mustard-seed, half pound of whole allspice, one-eighth of a pound of cloves; chop the cabbage, sprinkle salt well through, and put under a weight; pour the water off when it is pressed out; chop up the peppers, and add them to the cabbage. Boil the spices and seeds in the vinegar. Tie the spices in a bag. When cold, pour the vinegar all over the cabbage.

POTTING.

"In England potting is an every-day affair for the cook. If there be ham, game, tongue, beef, or fish on the table one day, you are quite sure to see it potted on the next day at lunch or breakfast. It is a very good way of managing left over food, instead of invariably making it into hashes, stews, etc. These potted meats will keep a long time. They are not good unless thoroughly pounded, reduced to the smoothest possible paste, and free from any unbroken fibre."

POTTED CHICKEN, AND TONGUE OR HAM.

Roast the chicken, take off all the meat, separating it from the sinews, and skin, chop and pound thoroughly with a pound of tongue or ham. Let the bones of the chicken be boiled down to a glaze, moisten the pounded meat with this glaze, season with salt, cayenne pepper, nutmeg, and a piece of butter. When well pounded in a mortar to a paste, put it into pots, with some boiling water in the bottom; let them be steamed half an hour and then let them cool. Press the meat down again, wipe dry and cover with some hot butter. It will keep for months.

PLAS EYTON POTTED HAM.

Mince some cold cooked ham, mixing lean and fat together; pound in a mortar, seasoning at the same time with cayenne pepper, and powdered mace, and mustard. Put into a dish and place in the oven; half an hour afterwards pack it in small stone jars, and cover with a layer of clarified butter, luke-warm, and tie bladders or paste paper over them. Leftover meat may be potted in the same way; chop the meat well cooked, and pound with butter, salt, pepper, and mace; prepare as for potted ham.

MORECAMBE POTTED HERRINGS.

Scale them and take off the heads and tails, and with the head and gills draw out carefully a string that runs through the body, letting the roe remain; wipe them dry and pack them in a stone pot, and between every layer of fish strew a mixture of salt, black pepper, ground allspice and cloves, adding some whole pepper and allspice. Cover them with vinegar, and lay a plate on top of the fish to keep them down. Cover the pot with dough and put in the oven, when the oven is cooling after a bread baking. Let them remain until the oven is cold. If a second plate is put on top, it prevents the dough falling.

NEW BRIGHTON POTTED LOBSTER.

Put the lobster in boiling water, and let it boil for half an hour; then pick all the meat from the body and claws, and beat it in a mortar; add nutmeg, mace, cayenne and salt to the taste; beat the coral separately; then put the pounded meat into a large potting-can, with a cover; press it down hard, having arranged it in alternate layers of white meat and coral, to give it a marbled appearance; cover it with fresh butter and put it in a slow oven for half-hour. When cold, take off the butter and clarify it by putting it into a jar, which must be set in a pan of boiling water; put the lobster into small potting-cans, pressing it down very hard; pour the clarified butter over it, and secure the covers tightly. Potted lobster is used to lay between thin slices of bread as sandwiches.

POTTED TONGUE.

One pound of boiled tongue, six ounces of butter, some cayenne, small spoonful of mace, nutmeg and cloves, each half a teaspoonful; the tongue must be unsmoked, boiled and skinned; pound it in a mortar as fine as possible, with the spices; when well blended, press the meat into small potting-pans, pour over it clarified butter, luke-warm, and tie bladders, or paste paper over them. A small quantity of roast veal, or the breast of turkey or chicken added is an improvement.

INDEX.

Albany Cake	78
Angels' Food	86
Apple Custard	61
" Dumplings	61
" Preserve	89
" Sauce	51
Artichokes, To Boil	44
Asparagus Soup	5
Bag Pudding	61
Batter Pudding	62
" " Suet	62
Bean Soup	5
" Black or Turtle	6
Beef, A la Mode	20
" Broiled, Devilled	38
" Cakes	38
" Cannelure of	38
" Fillet of	21
" " with Sauce	22
" Kidney, Fried	23
" Roast	20
" Salting	22
" Tea	6
Berry Pudding	62
Boston Sauce	53
Brain Cakes	40
Bread Pudding, Boiled	62
" " Arcadian	63
Breakfast Cakes	48
" Rolls	48
Broil Fish, To	18
Brown Betty Pudding	63
Brown Sauce	52
Buns, Franklin	79
Calf's Head, Baked	27
" To Prepare	26
" or Mock Turtle Soup	9
Calf's Liver, Roast	27
" Stewed	27
Caper Sauce	51
Caramel for Coloring Soups and Gravies	5
Cauliflower, To Boil	44
Celery Sauce	52
Cherry Pudding	64
Chicken Croquettes	33
" Potted	98
" Salad	46
" Spring	30
Chocolate Caramels	95
" Jumbles	86
" Pudding	64
" " Georgetown	66
Chow-Chow	96
Clam Fritters	14
" Soup	6
Cocoanut Balls	86
" Drop Cake	87
" Pie	57
" Sponge Cake	78
Codfish Balls	19
Cole Slaugh	47
Composition Cake	78
Confection, Domestic	95
Consommé Soup	7
Conserve, Lemon	71
Corn Bread	50
" Fritters	41
" Oysters	41
" Pudding	41
" Soup	8
Cottage Cheese Cake	56
" Pudding	64
Crabs, To Choose and Prepare	14
" Devilled	14
" Soft Shell	15
Cream for filling Cakes	71
Cream Sauce	54
Croquettes, Chicken	33
" Rice	33
" Rice for Meats	34
" Potato	34
" Veal	35
Crullers	79
Currant Jelly	93
" " Sauce	51

INDEX.

Custard Pudding, Orange	67
" Pie	57
" Frozen	77
Cutlets, Windham	24
Dandy Pudding	65
Doughnuts	60
Ducks, Roast	30
" Wild	30
Eggs, Scrambled	32
Egg Plant	45
English Plum Pudding	65
Fish, Broiled	18
Fish à la Russe	18
" Plain Fry	18
Fig Pudding	66
Floating Island	73
Fruit Cake	79
" Pudding, Boiled	63
Frozen Custard	77
" Peaches	77
German Sweet Sauce	54
Gelatine Jelly	93
Ginger Beer	94
Ginger-Bread, Hard	80
" Soft	80
" Southern Soft	80
" Shiny Backs	81
Ginger Nuts, Jingo	81
Green Gages, To Preserve	89
Hare, Jugged	29
Ham, Potted	98
Herring, Potted	99
Hominy, Boiled	45
Ice-Cream, Bisque	76
" Peach	76
Icing	88
" Boiled	88
Indian Pudding	66
Jumbles	87
Kaloola Cake	83
Lady Cake	81
Lamb, Broiled Shoulder of	24
Lawler's Dressing	46
Lake George Sauce	54
Lemon Pudding, Gordale	59
" Custard, Durentum	57
" Pie, Long Branch	58
" " Mountain Lake	58
" " Merton College	58
Lincoln Pudding	67

Liver, Hashed	39
Lobster, Boiled	15
" Soup	8
" Potted	99
" Salad	46
Macaroon Custard	71
Maccaroni with Cheese	32
" Cheese	42
Malina Pie	40
Marble Cake	81
Mary's Cake	82
Marmalade, Orange	91
Maryland Biscuit	49
Minnesota Biscuit	49
Mint Sauce	51
Mince Meat	56
" Pie	59
Mock Turtle Soup	9
Mushrooms, Stewed	44
Muffins, Potato	50
No Name Cakes	87
Nut Kisses	87
Okra Gumbo Soup	9
Omelette, French	32
Oriental Mullagatawny Soup	10
Orange Custard Pudding	67
" Pudding	67
" Cake	82
" Marmalade	91
" Jelly	93
" Soufflé	72
" Water-Ice	76
" Pudding, St. Augustine	69
Oysters, Pickled	16
" Fried	16
Oyster Soup,	11
" Stewed	15
Ox Tail Soup	10
Ox Heart, Roast	22
" Stewed	22
Parker House Rolls	48
Pancakes	72
Pea Soup	11
" " Green	8
" " Split	13
" " " (Old)	12
Pepper Pot	12
Pepper Sauce	97
Peaches, Spiced	92
" Frozen	77

INDEX.

Peaches, Brandied	92
" " Boulevard	92
Plums, Spiced	92
Pennyghent Jumbles	87
Pie Crust, Plain	56
Pig, Roast a Sucking	28
Plum Pudding, English	65
Pumpkin Pie	59
Pudding Sauce	53
Pound Cake	82
Pork and Beans	42
Pop Overs	73
Potting	98
Potato Muffins	50
Potomac Sauce	55
Potatoes, Lyonnaise,	43
" Chips	43
" Croquettes	34
" Salad	47
Quail, to Cook	31
" " Truss	31
Queen Pudding	67
Quinces, Preserved	90
Raspberry Syrup	94
Rabbit, Jugged	29
Rice Pudding, Plain	68
" "	68
" Meringues	73
" Croquettes	33
" " for Meats	34
Rolly Polly	68
Roman Punch	77
Salmon, Boiled	19
Scones, Dropped	49
Snowflake Cake	83
Snow Pudding	68
Snapper, Stewed	17
Spring Chicken	30
Spanish Sauce, quick	52
" Cream	74
Sponge Cake	83
" " West End	84
" " Cream	84
Strawberry Cake	74
" Short Cake	75
" Sponge Cake	75
Strawberries, whole, to Preserve	90

Suet Pudding	69
Sweet Potatoe Pie	60
Sweet Breads, French Style	35
" " Larded	36
" " with Peas	35
Tapioca Pudding, Fruit	69
" Cream	75
Teal	30
Terrapin, Prepared	17
Tongue, Stewed	23
" Rolled	23
Tomatoes, Baked	43
" Preserved	91
" Catsup	96
" Green Pickles	96
Tongue, Potted	98
" "	100
Tripe	36
" Fried	36
Turkish Soup	13
Turkey, to re-cook	37
" Scalloped	37
Venison Steaks	29
Vanilla Sauce	54
Veal Croquettes	35
" Cutlets, Breaded	25
" Fricandeau of	25
" Rolled	26
" Minced	39
" Pressed	39
Vermicelli Pudding	70
Viennese Pudding	70
Velvet Cream	75
Waffles	50
Walnut Cake	84
Washington Cake	85
Water Ice, Orange	76
" " Lemon	76
" " Strawberry	77
" " Pine Apple	77
" " Roman Punch	77
White Potato Pie	60
" Cake	85
Wine Sauce	53
" " Royal	53
Wine Whey	94

MT. VERNON MARKET.

THE PLACE TO BUY YOUR
GROCERIES, MEATS, AND PROVISIONS,
—CARY'S CREAMERY BUTTER—

THOS. H. HARLAN,
South-east cor. Eighteenth & Mt. Vernon Sts., Philada.

J. C. HARMAN,
MANUFACTURER OF
UMBRELLAS AND PARASOLS,
—WALKING STICKS A SPECIALTY.—

1304 CHESTNUT ST., PHILADELPHIA.

FAIRMOUNT STEAM BAKERY.
A. J. MEDLAR CO.
(LIMITED,)

MANUFACTURERS OF FINE

CRACKERS, CAKES,
AND BISCUITS,

1428 to 1434 Fairmount Avenue,

PHILADELPHIA.

AUGUSTUS DAVIS,
BEEF BUTCHER,
BEEF OF THE FINEST QUALITY,

Stalls, 527 & 529 5th Av., Ridge Av. Farmers' Market,

RIDGE AVENUE AND EIGHTEENTH ST.

Marketing delivered free of charge.

WILLIAM SUTHERLAND,
Landscape and Jobbing Gardener,

Twenty-first Street, below Green,

Nurseries, 65th St. and Elmwood Av.

PHILADELPHIA, PA.

All work done in town and country on reasonable terms.

C. BROWN,
DEALER IN

GROCERIES AND PROVISIONS,
1813 Fairmount Avenue,

CORNER SHIRLEY,

PHILADELPHIA

All kinds of Fresh Meats and Country Produce in season.

F. M. BUSH,

N. E. cor. 17th & Wallace Sts.

GENERAL UPHOLSTERER.

FINE SPRING, HAIR, AND HUSK
MATTRESSES MADE TO ORDER.

LACE CURTAINS CLEANED AND STORED.

All kinds of Furniture Stored.

FURNITURE
RE-UPHOLSTERED, REPAIRED & OILED.

Furniture Covers and Slips made and fitted at short notice.

Upholstering and Jobbing of every description.

Carpets and Matting Sewed and Laid.

Verandah, Awning, and Window-Shade Manufacturer.

All kinds of Cabinets and Brackets on hand.

F. M. BUSH,
N. E. corner 17th and Wallace Streets,
PHILADELPHIA.

WIENER BROTHERS,
DEALERS IN
FINE FRUITS, NUTS & CONFECTIONERY,
Fancy Groceries,
Choice Italian, French and all Imported Wines,
FOR FAMILY USE.

1227 Chestnut Street, Philadelphia.

Confections, Holiday Novelties, German Favors, &c.
Fruits handsomely arranged in Baskets.

Wiener Brothers, 1227 Chestnut Street.

STEWART, PEIRCE & CO.
LACES,
EMBROIDERIES,
HANDKERCHIEFS.

Gents' Neck Wear and Notions.

The West-End Unlaundried Shirt a Specialty.

1416 Chestnut Street,

PHILADELPHIA.

The handy getting of things.

Never tire of congratulating yourselves, Philadelphians, on your markets; in which nearly everything for your bounteous larders is got under the cool shadow of one roof.

Here, too, you find under one roof, and on one floor, almost everything that people in other cities have to go for, in all weathers, from store to store, and from street to street. Did you ever think how much extra you could afford to pay for goods for such handiness of getting them?

And as you get good butter and fresh vegetables in the markets—good and fresh above the goodness and freshness known in most cities, New York for example—so here you get the best things in the whole world, if you like; in silks, dress-goods, bonnets, shoes, gloves, shirts; in short, in almost everything you deck your persons or furnish your homes with; and when you find our price for anything higher than somebody else's, let us know!

Our house is too big to be fine, and our visitors too many to be select; it is a big everybody's house; there are everybody's goods in it; and yours, no matter whether your purse is heavy or light. We welcome you all; we provide for you all; and we do not mean to provide meanly or thinly, or any way but bountifully.

The test of a merchant is, HOW BIG AND HOW TRUE A DOLLAR'S WORTH DOES HE GIVE?

JOHN WANAMAKER.

Chestnut, Thirteenth and Market Streets, and City Hall Square.

JOHN BORDEN & BRO.

MANUFACTURERS OF

GEORGE G. THOMAS' IMPROVED

Ventilators & Chimney-Tops,

(Patented July 11, 1871,)

FOR PRIVATE RESIDENCES, PUBLIC BUILDINGS, &c.

Also, Manufacturers of and Dealers in

HEATERS AND RANGES,

637 North Nineteenth Street, Philadelphia.

Joseph Allen,   *ESTABLISHED 1835.*   James C. Allen,
Henry W. Allen,   Joseph Allen, Jr.

Cabinet Makers & Upholsterers.

Interior Decorators.

ALLEN & BRO.

Medal Awarded 1876, International Exhibition.

1209 CHESTNUT STREET,

MANUFACTORY,   Philadelphia.
N. E. cor. 12th & Hamilton Sts.

SARAH C. WOOD'S
CONFECTIONERY,

1702 Mount Vernon Street,

PHILADELPHIA.

Cakes, Ice-Creams, Jellies, Meringues, Charlotte Russe,

&c. &c.

PARTIES AND WEDDINGS SUPPLIED.

H. HUTCHISON,
Apothecary,

Graduate of Philada. College of Pharmacy,

Fairmount Avenue & Twentieth St.

PHILADELPHIA.

P. E. CHILLMAN,

Formerly of P. E. Chillman & Co.

ARTISTIC PHOTOGRAPHER,

914 ARCH STREET,

PHILADELPHIA.

—Established 1860.—

JULIUS SICHEL,

DEALER IN

RIBBONS, SILKS AND VELVETS,

—MILLINERY GOODS—

105, 107 & 109 North Eighth Street,

PHILADELPHIA.

Trimmed Hats and Bonnets a specialty.

GEO. L. LUTZ,

MERCHANT TAILOR,

NORTH-WEST CORNER

RIDGE & FAIRMOUNT AVENUES

PHILADELPHIA.

JOHN WANAMAKER & CO.

"I say, Fred, where'd you get those trousers?"

"Where I get everything—why? but why weren't you over last night?"

"Never mind last night. I want to know about those trousers."

"You're too hard on a fellow—they're Wanamaker's kerseys, if you must know—but—"

"You don't mean those $3.50 kerseys?"

"I do exactly—if I like a thing I don't care how little I pay for it—do you?"

John Wanamaker & Co.

820 Chestnut Street.

HOWELL & BOURKE,

MANUFACTURERS OF

PAPER HANGINGS,

N. E. cor. Fourth & Market Streets.

FACTORY

Eighth St. & Snyder Avenue,

PHILADELPHIA.

First-class Paper Hangers sent to all parts of the country.

BARRETT & MARSHALL,
1914 FAIRMOUNT AVENUE,
Building and House-Furnishing
HARDWARE,
READY-MIXED PAINTS FOR FAMILY USE,
Putty and Glass, Fine Cutlery and Plated Ware.

HARRY C. BARRETT.   ROBT. L. MARSHALL.

AMERICA AHEAD!

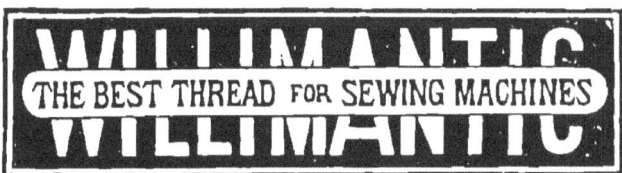
THE BEST THREAD FOR SEWING MACHINES

The Best Spool Cotton for Machines and Hand Sewing
IS THE
WILLIMANTIC,
New Six-Cord Soft Finish.
STRONG, SMOOTH AND ELASTIC.
Ask for the RED LABEL.

DIAMONDS.   *WATCHES.*

HAMRICK & SON,
JEWELERS,
804 Chestnut Street,

FINE JEWELRY.   PHILADELPHIA.   *SILVERWARE.*

Established 1841.

DAVID CARRICK & CO.

MANUFACTURERS OF

Crackers, Cakes, Biscuits, and Confectionery,

Nos. 1903 and 1905 Market Street,
PHILADELPHIA.

JOSEPH SLACK,

19th and Ridge Avenue,

AND

N. W. corner 17th and Fairmount Ave.

DEALER IN ALL KINDS OF

Groceries & Provisions.

FRESH MEATS AND VEGETABLES DAILY.

CHOICE ALDERNEY BUTTER.

PLUMBING AND GAS-FITTING

In all its branches promptly executed by

TOY & BRO.

929 Filbert Street, Philadelphia.

☞ Sewer-Gas Prevented.—Drains Laid.—Ventilation a Specialty.

All orders received at residence, 2002 Mt. Vernon Street, promptly attended to.—Charges low.

JAS. L. GRIEB,
MERCHANT TAILOR,
1518 Chestnut street,

Naval Uniforms.   PHILADELPHIA.

GAS FIXTURES.

THACKARA, BUCK & CO.
MANUFACTURERS OF
ARTISTIC GAS FIXTURES,
No. 718 CHESTNUT STREET,
PHILADELPHIA.

Continental Carpet Cleaning
AND
FIRE-PROOF STORE HOUSE,
(OUR NEW BUILDING,)

20th Street, above Chestnut Street, Philadelphia.

☞ 72 separate rooms for the storage of Furniture and Household Goods.

GRAND OPENING OF CHRISTMAS PRESENTS.

TOYS

FANCY GOODS AND NOVELTIES

In unsurpassed variety and extremely low prices.

G. A. SCHWARTZ,
1006 Chestnut Street, Philadelphia.

NEW STORE.

BUSH HILL.

NEW AND SECOND-HAND

FURNITURE

Bought and Sold.

S. E. CORNER

RIDGE AVE. & SPRING GARDEN STREET,

PHILADELPHIA.

All kinds of Furniture stored.

China and Cut Glassware neatly Riveted

BY
F. BENDIMERE,
818 Taney Street, Philadelphia.

Vases and other Ornaments Cemented.

The Extension of Cracks in Plate-Glass and China effectually Prevented.

GLEN ECHO MILLS.

McCALLUM, CREASE & SLOAN,

MANUFACTURERS AND IMPORTERS OF

CARPETINGS,

1012 & 1014 CHESTNUT STREET,

PHILADELPHIA.

WHITE BRONZE MONUMENTS

AND

CEMETERY ENCLOSURES,

ARE UNRIVALLED FOR

BEAUTY — ECONOMY — DURABILITY.

PAXSON, COMFORT & CO.

O. L. BILLINGS, Manager,

523 Market Street, Philadelphia.

Call or send for Illustrated Price List.

EARLES' GALLERIES.

816 Chestnut St. Philadelphia.

JAMES S. EARLE & SONS,
IMPORTERS AND MANUFACTURERS OF

Looking Glasses, Oil Paintings, Fine Engravings

Chromo-Lithographs, Picture-Frames.

AGENTS FOR THE CELEBRATED

ROGERS' GROUPS.

HOWSON & SONS,
SOLICITORS OF PATENTS,
AND
COUNSEL IN PATENT CASES,

Principal Offices, No. 119 South Fourth Street,
PHILADELPHIA, PA.

Branch Office, 605 Seventh Street, Washington, D. C.

L. KNOWLES.   C. P. PEROT.

L. KNOWLES & CO.
250 & 252 N. BROAD STREET, PHILADELPHIA,
Fine Family FLOUR a Specialty.

PILLBURY'S BEST,
HAMILTON'S FANCY,
GOLD MEDAL,
PLANT'S EXTRA,
} Agents for {
KING OF ALL,
RED STAR,
PATAPSCO,
STONEWALL.

CHAS. M. VANDEGRIFT,
BUILDING AND
HOUSE-FURNISHING
HARDWARE,
N. E. CORNER
Twentieth and Callowhill Streets,
PHILADELPHIA.

Mechanics' Tools, Cutlery, Nails and Sash-Weights
AT THE LOWEST MARKET PRICES.

HENRY J. SCHOCH,
LIVERY, SALE AND EXCHANGE STABLES,
640 North Sixteenth Street,
(Below Fairmount Avenue.)

Orders left at 728 Green st. will be promptly attended to.

☞ BOARDING HORSES A SPECIALTY. ☜

F. M. BUSH,

N. E. Cor. 17th and Wallace Streets,

General Upholsterer,

Verandah, Awning and Window-Shade Manufacturer.

All Kinds of Furniture Stored.

Upholstering and Jobbing of every description.

B. F. JARRETT,

Nineteenth and Brown Streets,

DEALER IN CHOICE

GROCERIES,

Fruits, Vegetables, Meats,

&c. &c.

Jackson Bros.

Railroad and Mercantile Printers,

400 & 402 Library Street,

Philadelphia.